I0080174

THE GOLDEN RULE: INTEGRATING SPIRITUALITY, RELIGION, AND LEADERSHIP

Exploring the Interconnection Between Inner Transformation, Belief, and Effective Leadership

Adeniran Koko, PhD, MBA

Global Quest Corporation

Copyright © 2025 Adeniran Koko

All rights reserved

No part of this book may be reproduced, or stored in a retrieval system, or transmitted in any form or by any means, electronic, mechanical, photocopying, recording, or otherwise, without express written permission of the publisher.

Published in the United States of America

To my beloved wife, Adebola, and children, Adelana and Adedunni Koko — you are my everything.

"Do to others as you would have them do to you." -Luke 6:31

"For the entire law is fulfilled in keeping this one command: "Love your neighbor as yourself." - Galatians 5:14

"And be good 'to others' as Allah has been good to you." - Quran 28:77

"… Refrain inflicting upon others such injury as would appear undesirable to us if inflicted upon ourselves. -Yogahastra 2:20

"Regard your neighbor's gain as your own gain: and regard your neighbor's loss as your own loss." - T'ai Shang Kan Ying P'ien

"Hurt not others with that which pains yourself." - Udana Varga 5:18
"In my spirituality… God loves Satan as much as God loves Mary and Jesus". -Participant 5

"Being spiritual, especially if your own spirituality teaches you love, compassion, and how to be selfless and help others, there is no way you won't be a better leader." -Participant 10

"But the fruit of the Spirit is love, joy, peace, forbearance, kindness, goodness, faithfulness, gentleness, and self-control. Against such things, there is no law." -Galatians 5:22-23

CONTENTS

PREFACE

For over three decades, I have been immersed in the dynamic world of research, science, operations, management, and consulting, a world where leadership styles paint the canvas of organizational success. I have witnessed firsthand the subtle yet powerful ways leaders shape their environments, influencing everything from daily operations to long-term strategic vision. But my curiosity always lingered beyond the surface, probing deeper into the wellspring of leadership decisions. This book represents a culmination of that curiosity, a journey that began with a simple question and evolved into a full-fledged doctoral exploration of the profound, often overlooked, influence of spirituality on leadership. My initial inquiry was deceptively simple: What truly drives a leader's decision-making process, especially when considering the role of their spiritual beliefs, or perhaps, the conscious absence of them? This question led me down a path of intricate exploration, delving into the deeply personal and often private realm of leadership.

Investigating this sensitive and nuanced aspect of human behavior presented unique challenges. The intimate nature of spirituality demanded a qualitative research approach, one that prioritized in-depth, personal conversations. This meant relying heavily on the generosity and candor of leaders willing to share their experiences and perspectives. I am profoundly grateful to every one of these courageous individuals who graciously volunteered their time and insights to participate in my doctoral research. Their invaluable contributions form the very foundation upon which this book is built, providing the rich tapestry of real-world examples and reflections that bring the research to life. Their openness allowed me to explore the subtle ways in which spiritual values, or the lack thereof, can permeate every facet of leadership, from ethical considerations and strategic choices to the cultivation of organizational culture and the fostering of employee morale.

This project, from its inception to its final form, has been a collaborative endeavor. I extend my sincere gratitude to the many individuals who generously contributed their time, expertise, and support to the refinement of this work. Their insightful feedback, careful reading, and constructive critiques were instrumental in shaping the final manuscript. I am particularly indebted to Ayodeji Olawunmi, Osei Charles, Dr. Taiwo Ayodele Ajayi, Modupe Olaiya, Wole Bakare, and Samuel Omolewu for their invaluable contributions. Their diverse perspectives and thoughtful suggestions challenged me to think more deeply about the implications of my research and helped me to craft a narrative that is both academically rigorous and accessible to a wider audience. They helped me to see the forest for the trees, ensuring that the book not only presented the data accurately but also conveyed the human stories and experiences that lay at its heart.

Within these pages, I invite you to join me in this exploration of the fascinating and often complex interconnection between spiritual traits, faith, and leadership. While the book maintains a level of academic rigor, incorporating scriptural references and established research to triangulate and validate the findings derived from the data, I encourage you to engage with it with a semi-academic mindset. My primary aim is not simply to present research findings, but rather to ignite a thoughtful conversation about the often-unseen forces that shape leadership decisions and, consequently, influence the world around us. I believe that understanding these deeper influences can empower us to become more effective leaders ourselves and to create organizations that are not only successful but also aligned with our core values.

Thank you for joining me on this journey of discovery.

Adeniran Koko, PhD, MBA, MS, PMP, ASCP, MLS,LBBP, ACC

INTRODUCTION

In a world often characterized by chaos and uncertainty, effective leadership has never been more critical. The Golden Rule: Integrating Spirituality, Religion, and Leadership explores the profound connection between spirituality, faith, and the core tenets of effective leadership. This book delves into the transformative power of leading with empathy, integrity, and purpose. By examining the alignment between personal beliefs, inner growth, and impactful leadership, this book uncovers how a strong spiritual foundation can shape authentic and effective leaders.

Through the lens of the Golden Rule, a universal principle found in various religious and philosophical traditions, the book explores how ethical, compassionate leadership can foster positive change. By drawing on practical insights, personal stories, and actionable advice, this book offers a roadmap for modern leaders to align their values with their actions, deepen their faith, and create a lasting, positive impact on their organizations and communities. By understanding the psychological dimensions of spiritual leadership and the role of spirituality in various leadership styles, we can unlock the potential for more compassionate, ethical, and effective leadership.

Leaders hold immense significance as they represent the face and identity of their group, organization, or even a nation, and decisions made by leaders can determine the fate of the people they guide, making the quality of leadership crucial for survival, profitability, and success of any endeavor. Therefore, understanding the mindset, cognition, attitude, behavior, and perception of leaders becomes paramount, but even more critical is grasping the unique innate qualities that shape each leader's decision making, identity, and true self.

The self, that inherent essence of who we are, is closely tied to a person's spirituality. Yet, the connection between a leader's spirituality and their approach to leadership remains elusive. This enigma became the focal point of my doctoral thesis, where I delved into the role of spirituality in the leadership styles of organizational leaders and this book builds upon that academic research work. Through interviews and qualitative analysis, I uncovered how leaders integrate their spirituality into decision-making, communication, and vision, and by weaving these findings with insights from psychology, management, and faith traditions, this book offers a fresh perspective on how leaders can align their values with their actions. In exploring this dynamic intersection, this work considers how leaders grounded in spiritual beliefs navigate the ethical and practical challenges of their roles.

Spirituality provides a wellspring of resilience, clarity, and purpose, equipping leaders to inspire others while navigating adversity. However, it also raises questions: How do leaders reconcile their personal convictions with organizational demands? How do spiritual beliefs influence decision-making in diverse, sometimes secular environments? Drawing on theories such as Leon Festinger's cognitive dissonance and Henri Tajfel's social identity, this book attempts to answer these questions by exploring how leaders integrate their spirituality with their professional roles. It examines how they align their faith with their leadership style, fostering authenticity and ethical clarity in the process.

This book also shares real-life stories of leaders from diverse backgrounds, offering practical insights and reflections. Through their experiences, readers will discover how spirituality can enhance leadership effectiveness, deepen self-awareness, and inspire positive change. By the end of this journey, readers will gain a deeper understanding of the interplay between spirituality and leadership and how personal transformation can lead to impactful, values-driven leadership. Whether you are an established leader, an aspiring one, or simply someone seeking to merge personal beliefs with outward influence, this book provides tools and inspiration to lead with authenticity, empathy, and purpose - creating a legacy of integrity and compassion.

CHAPTER ONE

Spirituality Overview

I have always been intrigued by the true essence of spirituality. Like many, I have often conflated it with concepts like religion and faith. Even scholars struggle to agree on a single, definitive explanation, making it even more challenging to define. In this book, you'll explore various interpretations of spirituality and what it means to different individuals.

Simon Cassar and Pnina Shinebourne, for instance, characterize spirituality as distinctive practices that signify a belief in a higher being or the universe. Kelly Phipps, in a similar vein, perceives spirituality as "the human yearning for connection with the transcendent, the quest to unify the self into a coherent whole, and the realization of one's latent potential." Louis Kavar echoes this sentiment, portraying spirituality as a state of positivity and pure experience. Carlos Del Rio and Lyle White define spirituality as an attitude towards life, a way of making sense of life, relating to others, and seeking unity with the transcendent. Rafik Beekun and James Westerman portray spirituality as the innate drive to uncover deeper meaning in life. For me, I see spirituality as the journey to connect with a higher power by aligning your thoughts, words, and actions with that power, hoping to receive blessings or forgiveness in return. The word spirituality is employed in a myriad of ways, but for me, it denotes a sense of linkage with something greater than oneself, a perception of interconnectedness with all things, and an expedition in search of meaning and purpose in life.

Sukumarakurup Krishnakumar and Christopher Neck posit that the highly personal and individualistic nature of spirituality is the very reason behind the disparities in its descriptions, which, in my view, accounts for the absence of a consensus in its definition. Despite this lack of consensus, certain terms consistently resurface in the description of spirituality, encompassing interconnectedness, the pursuit of meaning and purpose, and the occurrence of unique life events. Helen Astin offers a comprehensive take on spirituality by asserting, "Spirituality concerns the values we cherish most deeply, our sense of identity and origins, our convictions about our purpose - the meaning and significance we find in our labor and existence - and our feeling of interconnectedness with both one another and the world that surrounds us." Astin further notes that spirituality involves deeply personal experiences that are often arduous to articulate or communicate to others.

These definitions collectively emphasize that spirituality is personal and unique, propelling individuals toward behaviors that lead to an experience of purpose, a meaningful existence, and a profound connection with the sacred, transcendent, or divine. Spirituality is also entwined with notions of inspiration, intuition, mysteries, and mysticism, setting it apart from religion, with which it is frequently conflated.

While spirituality is often linked to religious beliefs and practices, it transcends any religion or belief system. It is a deeply personal and subjective encounter, shaped by an individual's cultural, social, and historical background. The exploration and nurturing of spirituality offers numerous benefits. Research has demonstrated that spirituality can positively influence mental and physical health, as well as emotional well-being. It has been associated with diminished stress, anxiety, and depression, in addition to fostering improved physical health outcomes, such as reduced blood pressure and a decreased risk of heart disease. Moreover, spirituality can facilitate personal growth and self-discovery. By forging a connection with something beyond oneself, individuals gain a sense of purpose and meaning in life and acquire deeper insights into their identity and values. This leads to heightened self-awareness and a more profound comprehension of one's place in the world. Furthermore, spirituality can cultivate a sense of community and belonging, uniting individuals who share similar beliefs and perspectives. This fosters a stronger sense of connection and support, enabling individuals to feel part of a greater whole.

To put it succinctly, spirituality is an intricate, multifaceted concept that can profoundly impact one's life. Whether through religious rituals, meditation, or simply by connecting with the natural world, spirituality offers individuals a sense of purpose and meaning, contributing to enhanced mental and physical well-being, a deeper sense of community, and an increased awareness of self.

SPIRITUALITY AND THE SELF-CONCEPT

In the realm of self-exploration, it becomes evident that the self extends far beyond one's physical reflection in the mirror. This multifaceted concept continues to captivate the curiosity of social scientists and psychologists who have devised various theories to elucidate its intricacies. The self-concept, as postulated by Jeremy Abel, Cheryl Buff, and John O'Neill, serves as the amalgamation of all that an individual believes about themselves. In essence, the self can be defined as one's perception of their own image or succinctly put, as the cumulative assessment of oneself.

The interplay between self-concept and self-esteem causes behavioral transformation, a process referred to as self-presentation. Many individuals grapple with their self-image and employ self-presentation to align their self-image with the perceptions of others. Put simply, self-presentation is the method through which individuals endeavor to influence the opinions and thoughts of others about themselves. It is on the foundation of this concept of self-presentation that someone identifying as spiritual may seek to harmonize their self-image with their spiritual beliefs, thereby minimizing cognitive dissonance as proposed by the cognitive dissonance theory and fostering identification with like-minded individuals as suggested by the social identity theory. Bella DePaulo, in her study of self-presentation and nonverbal behaviors, describes self-presentation as the tendency to convey an impression to others that may not align with one's own self-perception. This is relevant for leaders, who may need to project a particular image to employees and customers that differs from their personal identity. They may also present themselves differently spiritually due to the need to separate their personal spirituality from the professional sphere which could impact their psychological wellbeing.

Psychological studies indicate that one's sense of self and self-worth greatly relies on self-presentation. This is a way to fulfill personal identity growth and gain higher levels of acceptance, respect, and self-esteem. This practice is frequently crucial in leadership positions, playing a vital role in uplifting morale and effectively managing work-related pressures. Samina Awan and Aisha Sitwat assert that workplace spirituality and self-esteem play pivotal roles as predictors of psychological well-being. Self-esteem, in this context, is viewed as an integral component of the self, determining how individuals evaluate themselves on a positive-to-negative spectrum. Consequently, the psychological well-being of organizational leaders is intricately interwoven with their self-esteem and their ability to express their spirituality, or the alignment of their leadership style with their spiritual beliefs. Julie Kaplan characterizes self-esteem as the level of contentment and confidence an individual has in their own being. So, leaders who are unable to express their spirituality may experience low self-esteem and, consequently, diminished psychological well-being. This, in turn, may lead to behavioral adjustments, as postulated by psychological theories such as social comparison, self-discrepancy, and social perception theories, among others.

Spirituality and the self both share a profound connection, as spirituality can wield a transformative impact on an individual's sense of identity and self-awareness. Spirituality can be described as the perception of a connection to something greater than oneself, encompassing a quest for meaning and purpose in life. This pursuit for connection to something greater than oneself motivates individuals to explore their values, beliefs, and experiences, providing a framework to comprehend their place in the world. Not surprisingly, research has demonstrated that spirituality plays an instrumental role in personal growth and self-discovery. By establishing a connection with something beyond themselves, individuals gain a profound sense of purpose and meaning, fostering a deeper understanding of their own identity and values. This process of connection also leads to heightened self-awareness and a more profound understanding of one's place in the world. Moreover, spirituality can also instill a sense of belonging and community, as individuals with similar values and perspectives come together to share their beliefs and experiences. This sense of community offers vital support and connection, essential for personal growth and self-discovery.

Spirituality exerts a positive influence on mental and emotional well-being. Research reveals its capacity to mitigate stress and anxiety, enabling individuals to navigate life's challenges with resilience. It can bestow a sense of purpose in life, contributing to increased life satisfaction and a more optimistic outlook on the future. Spirituality manifests in diverse forms and is accessible through various practices, such as meditation, prayer, mindfulness, and the appreciation of the natural world. In the realm of spiritual exploration, one can discern spirituality as the profound connection between one's inner essence or the self and the transcendent or divine, achieved through transformative behaviors like devotion and meditation, ultimately elevating one's self-esteem.

In essence, spirituality represents a pivotal facet of the self, reflecting personal beliefs, experiences, or the sense of being interconnected with the transcendent or the divine.

Put simply, spirituality and the self are intricately intertwined, with spirituality emerging as a pivotal factor in personal growth and self-discovery. By establishing a connection with something greater than oneself and exploring values and beliefs, individuals can achieve a deeper understanding of their identity and their place in the world which also leads to greater well-being and life satisfaction.

SPIRITUALITY VERSUS RELIGION

The concepts of spirituality and religion, although often used interchangeably, are fundamentally distinct. While religion encompasses structured beliefs and practices, spirituality delves into a personal, individual experience rooted in a connection with something greater than oneself. This connection can indeed spring from religious beliefs, but it can also emanate from a multitude of sources, encompassing nature, art, and personal relationships.

Religion typically entails an organized set of beliefs, rituals, and practices designed to bring individuals closer to a higher power or ultimate truth. This might involve attending religious services, engaging in prayer or meditation, and adhering to specific moral or ethical guidelines. Religion is often passed down from generation to generation and provides a sense of community and belonging to its adherents.

In contrast, spirituality is a highly personal and individualistic experience, often unique to each person. It revolves around the connection with something greater than oneself and can draw inspiration from a diverse range of sources, including religious beliefs, nature, art, or personal relationships. Unlike religion, spirituality generally doesn't involve structured beliefs or practices and is not tied to any specific religious or cultural tradition.

However, there is often a considerable overlap between these two concepts. Many individuals discover that their spiritual experiences are deeply intertwined with their religious beliefs and practices. In turn, their religious beliefs can furnish a framework for comprehending these spiritual encounters. Likewise, spiritual experiences can significantly impact religious beliefs and practices, deepening the connection to one's religion.

While both concepts share a connection to the transcendent, they diverge in their approach. Religion adheres to structured and dogmatic worship of the transcendent, while spirituality forms the foundational basis upon which religion is built. Kavar characterizes religion as dogmatic and ritualistic, often entailing affiliation with religious institutions or practices. Religion can be perceived as a personalized or organized mode of connecting with the sacred, ultimately becoming the identity and mode of worship for a group. On the contrary, Kavar stated that spirituality is an inherent dimension of human experience, expressing itself subtly through actions, behaviors, and religious practices.

Religious activities can evoke profound spiritual experiences, such as trance-like states, feelings of euphoria, and even sensations resembling out-of-body experiences. The way these experiences are understood often depends on a person's religious beliefs and practices. However, these spiritual experiences are not limited to any particular religion, as they appear to be intrinsic to human nature. This aligns with the study by Del Rio and White, which suggests that "individuals are born spiritual, not religious."

THE INTERPLAY BETWEEN SPIRITUALITY AND DNA

The study by Del Rio and White suggested that humans may be innately wired for spirituality. The outcome of this study suggests that there may be a relationship between spirituality and human DNA. The relationship between spirituality and DNA is a fascinating topic that bridges the realms of science and spirituality with some researchers suggesting that there might be a genetic component to spirituality. For instance, geneticist Dean Hamer proposed the existence of a "God gene" that influences a person's inclination towards spirituality. This gene is associated with a personality trait called self-transcendence, which is linked to spiritual experiences.

Epigenetics studies how environmental factors can influence gene expression. This field suggests that spiritual practices, such as meditation and prayer, can potentially affect our genes by turning certain genes on or off which means that our spiritual experiences and practices might have a tangible impact on our biology. Some people even believe that DNA may be spiritual. Beyond the biological aspect, they view DNA as a metaphorical bridge between our physical existence and our spiritual essence. This perspective sees DNA as embodying resilience, evolution, connectivity, and potential. While genetics might play a role, cultural transmission is also crucial. Spiritual beliefs and practices are often passed down through generations, shaping our spiritual outlook and experiences.

The interplay between spirituality and DNA is a complex and evolving field, blending scientific inquiry with profound philosophical questions about the nature of human existence. However, religion appears to have emerged after spirituality, evolving as a structured method of worship with most religious practices aligning with the cultural and lifestyle influences of their founders, adapting and spreading as people migrated, thus allowing these practices to grow and integrate into various societies.

UNDERSTANDING THE "SPIRITUAL BUT NOT RELIGIOUS" IDENTITY

In recent decades, the phrase "spiritual but not religious" (often abbreviated as SBNR) as described by Del Rio and White has gained remarkable traction. To better understand this concept, one needs to delve into the essence of what it means to identify as "spiritual but not religious," by examining the motivations, beliefs, and practices that shape the lives of those who embrace this identity. Often misunderstood or generalized, the SBNR identity represents a nuanced perspective in which people seek meaning, purpose, and a sense of connectedness beyond the bounds of organized religion.

SPIRITUALITY IN THE ABSENCE OF RELIGION

To understand why so many people today gravitate toward spirituality without religion, it is helpful to first unpack the terms themselves. Religion, in its traditional sense, is often seen as an organized system of beliefs, practices, rituals, and sacred texts, providing followers with a sense of moral framework, community, and shared history. Religions generally prescribe particular pathways to ultimate truth, deity, or enlightenment, often delineated by specific doctrines and hierarchies. Spirituality, on the other hand, is frequently defined as a broader quest for meaning and connection to something greater than oneself. This distinction between religion and spirituality is, however, not as clear-cut as it might seem, and many people experience an overlap between the two.

The rise of the SBNR identity reflects a growing dissatisfaction with institutionalized systems, especially where these systems fail to address the modern individual's need for personal agency, diversity of thought, and inclusivity. For many, the SBNR label allows them to explore their inner lives in ways that are more adaptable, intuitive, and often more inclusive of a broader array of beliefs and practices. In this context, spirituality is seen less as a structured set of rules and more as a personal journey—one that each person can tailor to their own understanding, experiences, and aspirations.

THE RISE OF THE SPIRITUAL BUT NOT RELIGIOUS IDENTITY IN MODERN SOCIETY

In modern society, the movement away from traditional religious frameworks can be attributed to several factors:

1. Decline in Institutional Trust: Many people today express skepticism toward institutions, including religious ones. Historical controversies, scandals, and rigid doctrines have alienated some, who feel that religious institutions fail to live up to their own ideals of compassion, inclusivity, and moral integrity.

2. The Influence of Individualism: The increasing emphasis on individualism in Western societies, particularly over the last century, has given rise to an ethos of self-discovery and self-definition. The SBNR identity often aligns with this drive, allowing individuals to forge unique spiritual paths free from traditional constraints.

3. Globalization and Access to Diverse Beliefs: Access to information and global travel has exposed people to a variety of spiritual practices from diverse cultures, such as meditation, mindfulness, yoga, and indigenous rituals. For many, a customized spiritual practice—one that may include elements from multiple traditions—feels more authentic and meaningful than adhering strictly to one established system.

4. Focus on Mental Health and Inner Well-being: Increasing awareness of mental health and wellness has led many to explore spirituality as a means of achieving personal growth, emotional balance, and resilience. Practices like mindfulness and meditation,

often framed as secular but rooted in spiritual traditions, have become central to many SBNR practices.

5. Desire for Inclusivity and Fluid Belief Systems: Many in the SBNR community are drawn to a worldview that allows for fluid beliefs, inclusivity, and growth. This perspective often values experience over dogma, encouraging individuals to remain open to change and new insights as they evolve in their understanding of spirituality.

CORE BELIEFS AND PRACTICES AMONG THE SBNR

While it's difficult to generalize, there are certain themes and practices that are common among those who identify as SBNR. The following elements provide a sense of what characterizes SBNR spirituality:

•   Seeking Personal Connection with the Sacred or Divine: The SBNR path frequently emphasizes personal experience with the sacred, whether understood as God, the Universe, cosmic energy, or simply a profound sense of interconnectedness with life itself. For many, this relationship is not mediated by religious authorities or clergy but is sought through meditation, self-reflection, nature immersion, and intuitive practices.

•   Belief in Universal Truths Rather than Fixed Doctrines: The SBNR community often believes that while individual religions offer valuable insights, they are all attempts to interpret the same ultimate reality. Many SBNR individuals embrace a syncretic view, taking wisdom from multiple sources without committing exclusively to one tradition.

•   Emphasis on Inner Transformation: Self-growth and transformation are central tenets for the SBNR, who often view spiritual practices as tools to improve one's capacity for love, empathy, resilience, and creativity. Activities such as journaling, dream analysis, yoga, and various forms of inner work become essential parts of a spiritual toolkit for personal evolution.

•   Connection to Nature and the Environment: A profound respect for nature is a common concept among many who identify as SBNR. For some, the natural world serves as a powerful teacher and sacred space for reflection, healing, and connection with the broader universe. This view often leads to an eco-spirituality that inspires reverence for the earth and an ethical commitment to environmental stewardship.

•   Open-Minded Exploration of Consciousness and Reality: Many SBNR individuals are interested in exploring consciousness, reality, and the mysteries of existence. This curiosity leads them to investigate areas like mysticism, psychedelics, meditation, and even scientific fields like quantum physics as potential windows into understanding the nature of life.

COMMON MISUNDERSTANDINGS AND CRITICISMS OF SBNR PEOPLE

Individuals who identify as SBNR (Spiritual But Not Religious) frequently encounter various misunderstandings and criticisms. Because spirituality without religion can seem ambiguous or even inconsistent to those from traditional religious backgrounds, it's sometimes dismissed as a superficial or "pick-and-choose" approach to spirituality. Critics contend that SBNR individuals may lack the depth, discipline, and structure that organized religion offers. They also argue that such individuals can be perceived as confused, rebellious, or simply aligning with contemporary societal trends.

Another common critique is that SBNR practices can become overly self-focused, emphasizing personal experience at the expense of communal values or ethical responsibility. While religion often provides a sense of community and ethical accountability, the highly individualistic nature of many SBNR paths can sometimes leave individuals without a structured sense of how their spiritual growth might serve others or contribute to society.

However, SBNR practitioners themselves often view these critiques as misunderstandings, asserting that spirituality without institutional bounds allows for greater authenticity and flexibility in their search for truth. Many feel that their approach allows for a more profound connection with the sacred by removing intermediaries and adhering less to doctrines that feel outdated or out of sync with their values.

Despite the highly personal nature of SBNR spirituality, the community still holds importance for many. SBNR individuals are often drawn to small, informal groups where they can explore their beliefs, share practices, and engage in discussions on spirituality without the pressure to conform. Retreats, workshops, and online communities have grown in popularity, providing spaces for like-minded individuals to connect. These gatherings create environments where people can meditate together, learn new techniques, or simply share their insights in a supportive setting. Though often temporary and lacking the structure of religious congregations, these communities can offer the camaraderie and shared purpose that organized religion traditionally provides.

The "spiritual but not religious" identity reflects a widespread and deeply felt yearning to connect with something beyond the material world, even as traditional religious affiliations decline. This shift doesn't represent a rejection of the sacred but rather a reimagining of how people can engage with it—on terms that feel more authentic, inclusive, and aligned with modern sensibilities. In a world of rapid change and diverse beliefs, the SBNR path illustrates a flexible and resilient approach to finding meaning, one that empowers individuals to seek out practices that resonate with their unique life experiences.

By embracing spirituality without institutional boundaries, SBNR individuals are shaping a new frontier of spiritual exploration that honors both individual autonomy and universal connection. Their path may lack some of the formal structure found in religion, but it is rich in personal significance and potential for growth—qualities that are, after all, at the heart of any authentic spiritual journey. The SBNR path may not be a new frontier as suggested by some, it may just be people going back to the very beginning of human existence when we were just spiritual, and religion had not yet been invented. This strong affinity for spirituality by SNBR individuals validates Del Rio and White's suggestion that "individuals are born spiritual, not religious."

People who identify as SBNR often lead in ways that are deeply influenced by their personal spiritual practices, emphasizing authenticity, compassion, mindfulness, and purpose. They tend to foster inclusive, collaborative environments where individuals are encouraged to explore their own paths and grow holistically. Their leadership style often emphasizes the importance of empathy, emotional intelligence, and the interconnectedness of all, helping to create spaces that are supportive, empowering, and growth oriented. While these are some common themes, it is important to remember that SBNR individuals come from diverse backgrounds and may exhibit a wide range of leadership styles. Ultimately, effective leadership for SBNR individuals is about authenticity, empathy, and a commitment to personal and collective growth which aligns to the golden rule.

◆ ◆ ◆

CHAPTER TWO

Understanding Leadership

In any group of people - whether in a family, a community, a workplace, or a social circle - someone inevitably steps into the role of leader. Sometimes this happens naturally, shaped by cultural norms or personal traits, while in other cases, leaders are chosen through formal processes like elections or appointments. The need for leadership is as old as humanity itself, and we see echoes of it even in the animal kingdom. Without effective leadership, groups often descend into chaos, their efforts collapsing under a lack of direction.

At its core, leadership is about influence. It is the ability to guide others toward actions and decisions that serve the greater good of the group. But true leadership isn't rooted in authority or control; it stems from qualities that inspire others to follow willingly. Great leaders don't depend on their titles - they earn trust through character, vision, and charisma. Leadership, ultimately, is about making a positive impact on the people around you.

Leadership involves motivating, inspiring, and guiding others with the goal of fostering a positive environment and achieving success for a group, organization, or institution. Carroll (2006) describes leadership as "a process of influence," meaning that leadership is about the ability to guide followers in ways that help the organization reach its goals. For leadership to be effective, the relationship between leaders and followers must be positive and mutually beneficial. This dynamic, built on trust and cooperation, allows leadership to be shaped by deeper influences.

According to Carroll, leadership can be either formal or informal. A formal leader is someone appointed to a leadership position, while an informal leader influences others without an official title or position. Regardless of the type of leadership, there are certain traits that many leaders share. These include self-confidence, vision, intelligence, passion, integrity, responsiveness, resilience, motivation, teamwork, effective communication, interpersonal skills, and a desire to lead. In simple terms, leadership is personal and shaped by each person's unique qualities, which is why everyone has their own way of leading.

LEADERSHIP STYLES

Leadership style is a distinctive management methodology employed by individual leaders in their day-to-day organizational stewardship. It is highly individualistic, varying from person to person, and encompasses well-known styles like autocratic, laissez-faire, paternalistic, democratic, servant leader, transformational, and transactional leadership, among others. Nevertheless, Alice Eagly and Blair Johnson have introduced the simpler and more comprehensive Interpersonal-oriented and Task-oriented leadership styles. These styles are unique in that they encompass a broader spectrum of leadership behavior compared to some other styles. They are rooted in an individual's inherent inclination to either focus on people (interpersonal-oriented) or the task at hand when fulfilling their leadership objectives, strategizing, or collaborating with subordinates and teams in executing a work plan. While numerous leadership styles have been defined, exploring the Task-oriented and Interpersonal-oriented leadership styles is particularly valuable as these encompass characteristics found in other styles, making them fitting umbrella models for the exploration of the role of spirituality in leadership.

TASK-ORIENTED LEADERSHIP

The Task-oriented leadership style, defined by Eagly and Johnson as a focus on accomplishing assigned tasks through the organization of task-relevant activities, is a leadership approach that centers entirely on the immediate job that needs to be completed. Leaders adopting this style are task-focused, channeling all their efforts and resources toward achieving specific goals and targets.

Task-oriented leaders are similar to the autocratic style in their unwavering focus on the task at hand. Much like autocratic leaders, those practicing Task-oriented leadership may be perceived as domineering, controlling, or even bossy. They often make decisions without seeking input or deliberation from their team members or employees. Unlike Interpersonal-oriented leaders, Task-oriented leaders tend to be less attuned to the needs of their employees, and their leadership style is characterized by limited communication, often resulting in a poor perception of workplace justice among employees.

Unlike Interpersonal-oriented leaders who strive to inspire and elevate their subordinates, Task-oriented leaders prioritize task completion over team dynamics. They are less inclined to foster a collaborative environment that promotes unity and camaraderie among employees. Their concern for employee well-being is often minimal, and they make little effort to accommodate personal needs. According to Carroll, this leadership style can lead to increased workplace stress, stemming from employee dissatisfaction with the domineering or dictatorial behavior of their leader. Task-oriented leaders frequently exhibit poor interpersonal and communication skills due to their relentless focus on the job at hand, leading to limited friendly and respectful socialization with their employees.

The benefits of Task-oriented leadership, much like the autocratic style, lie in its ability to achieve set goals, meet deadlines, and provide clear instructions for all employees. It ensures quick decision-making and task completion. However, it can also create a more hostile work environment. This style is similar to autocratic leadership in that it prioritizes productivity and the definition of team member roles over employee well-being. Task-oriented leaders foster success by setting clear deadlines and performance targets, resulting in well-defined goals and procedures, and expedited decision-making due to the leader's limited consultation with team members. Task-oriented leadership works well in professions like the military and other jobs where orders are required to be executed effectively and in a timely manner for success to be achieved. Unlike Interpersonal-oriented leadership, Task-oriented leaders do not typically exhibit personality traits associated with spirituality or adherence to the golden rule of treating others as they would like to be treated.

INTERPERSONAL-ORIENTED LEADERSHIP

The Interpersonal-oriented leadership style, also known as human-oriented or relationship-oriented leadership, as defined by Eagly and Johnson, is characterized by a focus on maintaining interpersonal relationships by nurturing the morale and welfare of others. The Interpersonal-oriented leadership style focuses on motivating, satisfying, and ensuring the overall well-being of team members. Leaders who adopt this style are also associated with promoting justice within their organizations, as highlighted by Panah, Sharifabadi, and Ardakani.

Leaders who embrace the Interpersonal-oriented style prioritize the inspiration and upliftment of their team members. They are often regarded as team players, fostering a collaborative atmosphere that emphasizes unity and camaraderie as much as task completion. These leaders display genuine concern for the welfare of their employees, striving to accommodate their personal needs and reduce workplace stress by minimizing conflicts among staff. They exhibit excellent interpersonal and communication skills by engaging with their employees in a humane and respectful manner. The Interpersonal-oriented leadership style encompasses characteristics of other relationship-based leadership styles, including democratic, servant, and transformational leadership styles, among others.

The selflessness and people-centered focus of leaders practicing the Interpersonal-oriented style often inspire employees to place the interests of the organization before their own. This behavior closely aligns with the attributes associated with the transformational leadership style, which Rafik Beekun and James Westerman suggest might be connected to spirituality. The emphasis on inspiration, motivation, and employee well-being draws parallels to spirituality since these terms are commonly intertwined with spiritual concepts. They also resonate with the universal "golden rule," which encourages treating others as one would wish to be treated.

In stark contrast to the Task-Oriented Leadership, this style prioritizes the development of relationships and the cultivation of a communal spirit among followers. Leaders embracing this approach exhibit a keen interest in the growth and advancement of their followers, motivating and inspiring them through their own exemplary conduct. They often radiate charisma and empathy, fostering open and honest communication with their followers. This style thrives in environments where collaboration, teamwork, and the nurturing of a positive organizational culture are paramount like in the sales and entertainment industries. However, it's essential to note that excessive people-centeredness can sometimes be distracting, diverting focus from the task at hand and potentially leading to reduced productivity and team efficiency.

Task-oriented and Interpersonal-oriented leadership styles have their own strengths and weaknesses. Effective leaders adapt their style to the context, blending both approaches to create inspiring and efficient leadership.

THE DYNAMIC NATURE OF LEADERSHIP STYLES

Leadership style is crucial, affecting an organization's profitability, culture, employee satisfaction, retention, and motivation. A leader's style can make or break an organization. When it aligns with the organization's goals, achieving success becomes easier.

Leaders who embrace the Interpersonal-oriented style tend to resonate with organizations that prioritize people, as seen in the entertainment industry, where building relationships and morale among team members is paramount. Conversely, the Task-oriented leadership style is better suited to organizations where work plans demand precision and often entail repetitive tasks, exemplified by the military. Yet, there are environments and scenarios where leaders must fluidly transition between interpersonal-oriented and task-oriented leadership styles within the same organization or industry. For instance, military platoon leaders may rely on Task-oriented leadership in high-pressure combat situations but shift to Interpersonal-oriented leadership for daily interactions, fostering team morale and trust. Similarly, a leader in a theme park might transition from an Interpersonal-oriented style to a Task-oriented approach when executing specific projects that require clarity and structured execution.

This dynamism in leadership style is complex, as it necessitates behavioral adjustments, often requiring leaders to shift from their natural style to another style, contingent on the demands of the task at hand. Researchers have started to emphasize the behavioral aspect of leadership more than a specific style, recognizing that different leadership styles offer unique strengths and weaknesses. In this light, the focus of leadership studies has evolved to delve into leadership behavior and personality traits.

LEADERSHIP STYLE AND PERSONALITY TRAITS

Human behavioral tendencies have long fascinated researchers, with William Marston's pioneering work shedding light on the four intrinsic motivators that underpin human emotions. These motivators gave birth to the - Dominance, Influence, Steadiness, and Conscientiousness (DISC) - personality types. The DISC profile has since become a valuable tool, providing insight into human behavior. This profile is often used to assess individual strengths, particularly within the realm of leadership.

Individuals displaying the Dominance (D) personality type are often result-focused, competitive, and direct, similar to the task-focused orientation of the Task-oriented leadership style. On the other side, those with an Influence (I) personality type tend to be people-focused, independent, and optimistic. Similarly, the Steadiness (S) personality type leans towards being cooperative, sympathetic, and helpful, reflecting a people-focused orientation akin to Interpersonal-oriented leadership. In contrast, individuals with a Conscientious (C) personality lean towards the task-focused domain, aligning with the Task-oriented leadership. Much like leadership styles, DISC profiles are contingent upon an individual's natural or adopted style and personality. A leader's natural style is intrinsic, creating harmony when it aligns with the policies and procedures they must implement. However, individuals who adopt a leadership style that deviates from their personality traits or spiritual beliefs—whether due to training, job requirements, or external factors—may find it unnatural, leading to personal struggles and cognitive dissonance which may impact their mental health and emotional wellbeing.

Personality traits and leadership style aren't standalone elements. They intricately interact with a leader's traits often guiding the adoption of a particular leadership style. A confident leader, for instance, may naturally gravitate towards a directive and dominant, Task-oriented approach, whereas a more introverted leader might embrace a supportive Interpersonal-oriented style. Leadership style and personality traits are integral components that significantly influence a leader's behavior and effectiveness. Understanding how these factors intersect empowers leaders to develop a leadership approach that plays to their strengths while meeting the unique needs of their followers.

◆ ◆ ◆

CHAPTER THREE

Spirituality and Leadership

L eadership is commonly perceived as a set of skills and competencies that enable individuals to effectively guide and inspire others. Nevertheless, recent research underscores a compelling link between spirituality and leadership, emphasizing the pivotal role of inner transformation and personal growth in effective leadership. Spirituality, by definition, encompasses a connection with something greater than oneself and can encompass various beliefs and practices, including religious faith, meditation, and mindfulness. This inner transformation holds the potential to enhance self-awareness, empathy, and a deeper understanding of one's values and purpose. Consequently, these aspects can significantly bolster one's leadership capabilities.

One of the most prominent ways through which spirituality influences leadership is the cultivation of empathy. Spirituality often accentuates compassion and the well-being of others, thereby shaping a leadership style that places the needs of followers at the forefront. This heightened empathy not only fosters trust but also nurtures positive team dynamics by enabling leaders to connect with and comprehend their team members more effectively. Another significant avenue through which spirituality informs leadership is the development of self-awareness and personal insight. Spiritual practices often encourage introspection and self-reflection, leading to a more profound comprehension of one's values, beliefs, and motivations. This heightened self-awareness subsequently guides leadership decision-making, ensuring alignment with personal values and beliefs. Numerous spiritual practices emphasize the quest for life's purpose, offering leaders a clear sense of direction and motivation. This sense of purpose not only serves to inspire and motivate others but also guides leaders in making decisions consistent with their deeply held values and beliefs.

Workplace spirituality, as highlighted by Krishnakumar and Neck, yields numerous benefits, including increased individual creativity, intuition, heightened awareness, improved honesty, trust, personal fulfillment, commitment, and overall organizational performance. Zwart and Astin propose a connection between spirituality and the transformational leadership style, as linking what we do with our inner selves forms the bridge between spirituality and leadership. Consequently, leaders who are spiritual may experience limitations imposed by policy and job constraints, which may lead to dissonance and, ultimately, psychopathology or mental health issues.

Psychological research, as well as other fields, corroborates the role of spirituality in the workplace. Lips-Wiersma and Mills assert that spirituality is already present, with many individuals holding spiritual beliefs but struggling to articulate or enact these beliefs at work. Thus, organizational leaders may already be covertly influenced by their spiritual beliefs in making business decisions, thereby minimizing dissonance associated with conflicting values. Therefore, it is vital to comprehend the experiential dimension of spirituality and psychology, as behavior influences leadership style, which, in turn, shapes worker satisfaction, retention, and motivation.

The role of spirituality in leadership extends across various spheres of business and society. Leadership decision-making, a critical aspect of leadership style, has been shown to be influenced by personal religious biases and spiritual beliefs as seen in the decision by organizations like Chick-fil-a to close on Sundays. The influence of spirituality on the behavior and political decisions of political leaders has been well-documented. Candidate electability in the United States, particularly in the so-called "bible belt," has historically been significantly influenced by candidates' religion or spirituality. Spiritual beliefs have also played a pivotal role in national debates on issues such as marriage equality, abortion, and politicians' religious affiliations. Despite the principle of the separation of church and state, issues related to spirituality, including abortion, family composition, and sexuality, have emerged as significant topics in American politics, with the politically conservative leaders advocating for regulations in line with their spiritual beliefs, morality, and sacred principles. So, personal spirituality remains a pivotal but often unspoken influence on government, the workplace, and business or political decision-making.

As described, leadership is the art of motivating, inspiring, and guiding subordinates with the aim of fostering a positive environment and achieving success for the institution or organization one serves. It can be described as a process of influence, wherein leaders have the ability to inspire their followers to act in ways that advance the organization's objectives. For successful leadership, this interaction between leaders and followers must be characterized by positivity and reciprocity, which opens the door to spiritual influences.

As Burke (2006) noted, effective leadership is a multidisciplinary concept that goes beyond sociology, psychology, and technology, but also embracing spirituality. This implies that leadership is a pervasive and essential aspect of both society and organizations. Despite being central to the identities of many employees and leaders, spirituality is often considered taboo at the workplace, seen as divisive and distracting from the employer's perspective. However, employers have started advocating for employees to show up as their authentic selves at work ever since employers started getting reports of an increase in the number of employees expressing issues with their mental health. Despite this encouragement by employers for employees to be open about who they are, there are still some sensitivities to employees expressing their spirituality, beliefs, or overtly making business decisions that align with personal faith or spirituality.

Different religions have varying perspectives on spirituality and work. For example, Christians view spirituality as a calling to work for God, while Hindus see it as working with the highest devotion. Buddhists believe that dedication and hard work enrich one's life and benefit both the individual and the organization. Islam emphasizes commitment to one's organization, along with principles of justice and generosity at work, while the Taoists and Confucianists emphasize teamwork as a key aspect of spirituality in the workplace.

The information from leaders interviewed for this book suggests that leadership shares key characteristics with major spiritual and religious practices. These similarities can be valuable for managing work and leading groups or organizations effectively as shown in the key spiritual characteristics and best practices for effective leadership described below:

1. Vision and Strategic Thinking: A proficient leader possesses a well-defined vision of the future and effectively communicates this vision to their followers. They exhibit strategic thinking, considering both immediate and long-term objectives, and make decisions that uphold their organization's overall mission.

The intertwining of spirituality with leadership vision and strategic thinking is profound. Leadership vision entails envisioning the future and setting a course, while strategic thinking involves planning and executing steps to realize that vision. Conversely, spirituality often encompasses a sense of purpose, personal connection, and a broader worldview, significantly impacting how leaders approach their vision and strategy. Spirituality often fosters self-reflection and a deep understanding of one's values and purpose. Leaders attuned to spirituality are more likely to possess clear core values that shape their leadership vision. This clarity forms a robust groundwork for setting meaningful goals and crafting a compelling vision that resonates with both the leader and their followers.

Spirituality can play a role in shaping decision-making processes in leaders by highlighting ethical principles, compassion, and empathy. Those who integrate spiritual values tend to consider ethical implications beyond mere profit, guiding strategic decisions towards societal or communal welfare rather than individual gains. Leaders grounded in spirituality tend to possess more inclusive and inspiring visions. Their connection to a purpose beyond personal success enables them to articulate a vision that appeals to diverse groups. This inclusivity cultivates a sense of belonging and commitment among team members, fostering enhanced collaboration and productivity. Spirituality also provides a framework for resilience in confronting challenges. Spiritually inclined leaders often possess a broader perspective, enabling them to navigate setbacks with grace. This resilience aids in adapting strategies when faced with unexpected obstacles while keeping the overarching vision intact.

Furthermore, spirituality encourages a focus on sustainable, long-term outcomes. Leaders integrating spirituality consider the enduring impact of their actions on future generations, prioritizing sustainable practices and enduring success in their strategic thinking. A spiritually grounded leader excels in connecting with stakeholders on a profound level. They are adept at comprehending the needs and aspirations of their team, clients, and communities, enabling them to devise strategies that genuinely resonate. This fosters stronger relationships and loyalty among stakeholders.

In essence, spirituality acts as a guiding force that enriches a leader's vision and strategic approach. It encourages a holistic perspective, ethical decision-making, resilience, and authentic connections, all crucial elements in effective leadership. When spirituality merges with strategic thinking, it cultivates visionary leaders capable of inspiring, innovating, and steering organizations towards meaningful and sustainable success.

2. Emotional Intelligence: Proficient leaders adeptly navigate both their own and others' emotions, fostering effective communication, robust relationships, and a positive work atmosphere conducive to collaboration and innovation. The interplay between spirituality and emotional intelligence in leadership is intricate and consequential. Emotional intelligence encompasses the capacity to identify, comprehend, manage, and leverage emotions in oneself and others. Not to be confused with Emotional Quotient (EQ), Emotional intelligence is the broader concept that includes various emotional skills, while EQ is the metric used to assess those skills. In essence, EQ is a measure of a person's emotional intelligence.

Spirituality, often associated with a deeper sense of purpose, interconnectedness, and personal development, profoundly impacts a leader's emotional intelligence. Spirituality encourages introspection and self-awareness, enhancing a leader's understanding of their emotions, strengths, weaknesses, and motivations. This self-awareness lays the foundation for emotional intelligence, enabling leaders to acknowledge and manage their emotions effectively.

Spiritual practices offer frameworks for self-regulation and emotional equilibrium. Based on the research conducted for this book, leaders incorporating spirituality exhibited better emotional regulation, maintaining composure and thoughtfulness even in challenging situations, a pivotal aspect of emotional intelligence. Emphasizing empathy and compassion, spirituality equipped these leaders with a heightened sensitivity to others' emotions. This depth of empathy fosters authentic connections with team members, clients, and stakeholders, nurturing trust, and collaboration.

Spiritual principles promote harmony and cooperation.

Leaders integrating spirituality excel in relationship management, adeptly navigating conflicts, inspiring others, and fostering a supportive environment that encourages open communication and cooperation. Also, spirituality often involves mindfulness practices, fostering attentiveness and engagement. Leaders embracing such practices exhibit enhanced presence, facilitating active listening, nuanced understanding, and thoughtful responses, nurturing stronger connections.

In essence, spirituality contributes to leaders' resilience. Leaders who are grounded in spirituality can recover from setbacks and manage stress effectively. This aspect of emotional intelligence helps them to stay focused and lead efficiently during challenging times. Integrating spirituality with emotional intelligence in leadership fosters a holistic and authentic approach. This integration enables leaders to engage deeply with their own and others' emotions, creating an environment fostering trust, understanding, and growth. By blending spiritual principles with emotional intelligence, leaders cultivate workplace cultures valuing empathy, self-awareness, and meaningful connections, which ultimately enhances team performance and overall organizational success.

3. Authenticity: Proficient leaders epitomize authenticity, transparency, and steadfastness in their character. They articulate their values, beliefs, and objectives in a lucid and unwavering manner, ensuring congruence between their words and deeds. This cultivates trust and credibility among their followers. Also, the connection between spirituality and authentic leadership runs deep, with spirituality often guiding leaders to embody authenticity in their conduct, choices, and connections. Spiritual introspection often prompts a profound understanding of personal values and beliefs. The leaders interviewed for this book were deeply grounded in their spirituality, which shaped their actions around their core values. This helped them lead with integrity and stay committed

to their beliefs, even in challenging situations.

Spirituality champions authenticity through openness and transparency. Leaders embracing spiritual principles tend to be forthright about their thoughts, emotions, and intentions. This candidness fosters trust among team members, highlighting honesty and a genuine willingness to engage. Additionally, leaders with spiritual grounding often perceive vulnerability as a strength, not a weakness. They embrace authenticity and vulnerability, fostering an environment where others feel safe to be authentic. This culture of openness nurtures genuine connections and a supportive team dynamic.

Emphasizing empathy and attentive listening, spirituality influences authentic leaders to lend a sympathetic ear to others, comprehending their perspectives and emotions. This empathic approach strengthens genuine connections and cultivates a sense of mutual understanding within the team. As stated earlier, spiritually inclined leaders demonstrate consistency in behavior, upholding their values regardless of external pressures. This steadfastness contributes significantly to building trust and reliability, essential aspects of authentic leadership.

Spirituality frequently guides leaders towards a purpose-driven ethos. Authentic leaders, shaped by spirituality, anchor their decisions and actions in a broader purpose beyond personal gain. This purpose-oriented leadership inspires and motivates others, nurturing a shared sense of direction and significance. Authentic leadership, influenced by spirituality, doesn't imply inflexibility; it embodies adaptability. Leaders maintain fidelity to their core values while remaining open to growth, evolution, and learning. This adaptive authenticity facilitates leaders' evolution while preserving their genuineness and authenticity.

The fusion of spirituality and authentic leadership engenders a dynamic environment where leaders lead with sincerity, empathy, and a profound sense of purpose. These leaders foster inclusive settings where individuals feel acknowledged, understood, and valued, fostering a culture characterized by trust, innovation, and collaboration. Ultimately, the intersection between spirituality and authentic leadership empowers leaders not only to achieve organizational objectives but also to craft meaningful and impactful experiences for their teams and stakeholders.

4. Adaptability: Proficient leaders possess the agility to adapt swiftly to shifting circumstances and harbor comfort amidst ambiguity. Their ability to pivot strategies and make swift decisions upholds the quality of their leadership. The intricate relationship between spirituality and leadership adaptability resonates profoundly, shaping leaders' mindsets to navigate change, uncertainty, and challenges with resilience and an open perspective. It serves as a catalyst for embracing change as an inherent aspect of life and leaders influenced by spirituality often approach change with openness, perceiving it as an avenue for personal and professional growth, evolution, and enriching learning experiences. Rooted in spirituality, leaders cultivate inner resilience, equipping themselves to weather storms, overcome setbacks, and confront challenges with poise while remaining anchored to their core ethical values.

Championing a perpetual quest for knowledge and self-improvement, leaders embracing spirituality exhibit an open-mindedness eager to glean wisdom from fresh experiences. This receptivity fuels adaptability, allowing them to integrate novel insights into their leadership methodologies. Influenced by spirituality, leaders adopt a flexible approach to decision-making, receptive to diverse perspectives, and willing to recalibrate strategies based on emerging information. This adaptability empowers them to make swift decisions attuned to evolving contexts. Spirituality instills a sense of connection to a higher purpose within leaders, enabling them to perceive challenges through a broader lens. This holistic perspective empowers them to adapt strategies while remaining aligned with overarching goals and values. Leaders anchored in spirituality foster innovative environments. Their adaptability and openness to novel ideas create cultures that nurture creativity. They encourage experimentation and embrace creative approaches, sparking innovation within their teams and organizations. Their comfort with ambiguity and uncertainty, supported by spirituality, helps them manage unclear situations with calmness and clarity.

This adaptability empowers them to effectively guide their teams through times of uncertainty. The fusion of spirituality and leadership adaptability empowers leaders to traverse intricate and ever-evolving landscapes with resilience and grace. It enables them to perceive change as a springboard for growth, fostering cultures marked by continuous learning and innovation. Acting as a guiding compass, spiritual principles infuse leaders with an openness to change while remaining rooted in fundamental values. Ultimately, this integration empowers leaders to adapt, evolve, and flourish in dynamic environments, leading their teams with resilience and a steadfast commitment to meaningful solutions.

5.   Inspirational: Great leaders inspire and motivate their teams, creating a shared vision and sparking innovation. The bond between spirituality and inspirational leadership runs deep, fueling impactful leadership. Spirituality, linked to our inner values and a bigger picture of the world, greatly impacts a leader's ability to inspire others.

Spirituality often leads to deep thinking about what matters most to us. Leaders grounded in spirituality have a clear set of values and a strong sense of purpose. This helps them paint a compelling vision that resonates with their team, sparking inspiration. These leaders stay true to their beliefs, and that honesty builds trust among their team. When they live out their values, they motivate others to join in the vision. Spirituality also brings empathy and connection. These leaders genuinely care about their team's well-being, understanding what drives each person. This creates a sense of belonging and loyalty. They see beyond just success or money. Their vision is about something bigger, something meaningful. This vision inspires others to be part of something greater.

In tough times, spiritually grounded leaders show resilience and positivity. Their strength gives their team confidence and a fighting spirit. They practice servant leadership, putting their team's needs first which creates a supportive environment where everyone grows together. These leaders don't just talk the talk; they walk the walk. They lead by example, inspiring others to follow suit. Spirituality and inspirational leadership go hand in hand, creating an environment where leaders inspire through their actions, not just words. It builds a culture where people aren't just driven by goals but by a bigger purpose. Spirituality adds depth and purpose to leadership, empowering leaders to inspire and drive positive change among their teams and beyond.

6. Servant Leadership: Great leaders prioritize their team's needs and well-being, aiming for a balance between organizational goals and personal growth. The bond between spirituality and servant leadership, which is a form of the Interpersonal-oriented leadership style, runs deep, shaping a leadership approach that champions service, empathy, and the welfare of others. Spirituality often prompts deep self-reflection, leading to a stronger sense of self and a connection to something greater. This influence significantly shapes servant leadership, fostering a values-driven focus on serving others. For servant leaders influenced by spirituality, personal values align with the core principle of serving others. Their leadership is steeped in empathy, compassion, and a genuine desire to meet the needs of their team and wider community.

Driven by spiritually rooted empathy, these leaders genuinely care for those they lead. They actively listen, understand their team members' perspectives, and take actions that support their growth and success. Spirituality broadens the scope of leadership beyond personal gain. It inspires servant leaders to connect their purpose to a higher calling—serving others. It's not just about tasks; it's about making a positive impact on their team's lives. Humility and selflessness, encouraged by spirituality, define servant leadership. These leaders prioritize their team's needs, fostering an environment where everyone thrives and grows.

Drawing from a sense of interconnectedness nurtured by spirituality, servant leaders create a sense of community within their teams. They build an environment rich in collaboration, support, and respect.

Spirituality serves as a moral compass for servant leaders, guiding their decisions with values that prioritize the well-being of others. They embody the golden rule: treating others as they wish to be treated. They offer guidance and support, nurturing their team's growth and success. Servant leaders grounded in spirituality lead by example, embodying humility, empathy, and a commitment to serving others. Their actions inspire their teams to embrace similar values and behaviors. The blend of spirituality and servant leadership creates a style centered on service, fostering trust, support, and growth. It transcends mere management—it's a philosophy that transforms organizations into communities, where leaders are catalysts for serving and empowering everyone to thrive.

7. Accountability: Accountability plays a crucial role in effective leadership, serving as a foundation for trust, integrity, and transparency. It ensures that leaders are responsible for their decisions, actions, and the outcomes of their teams. When leaders hold themselves accountable, they set a positive example for others, fostering a culture of responsibility within the organization. Accountability also creates a system where leaders can be measured by their performance, helping to ensure fairness and ethical behavior.

Leaders who are accountable earn the trust of their teams, peers, and stakeholders. When leaders take responsibility for their actions, admit mistakes, and work to correct them, they demonstrate integrity and gain credibility. This trust is essential for a healthy and productive work environment, where team members feel secure and valued. Accountability pushes leaders to achieve high standards because they understand that they are responsible for meeting their goals. This drive for performance can spread through the team as leaders model the behavior they expect, encouraging team members to take ownership of their roles and outcomes. An accountable leader promotes transparency by openly sharing successes and failures. This transparency improves communication within the organization, reduces misunderstandings, and encourages a collaborative approach to problem-solving. Accountability requires leaders to think carefully about their choices, understanding that they will have to justify their decisions to their team and stakeholders. This responsibility leads to more thoughtful and strategic decision-making, minimizing risks and errors.

When leaders hold themselves accountable, they become more aware of their strengths and weaknesses. This self-awareness encourages continuous learning and personal growth, as leaders seek to improve their skills and leadership style. It also sets an example for others to follow, promoting a culture of self-improvement within the team. Leaders should establish clear goals and expectations for themselves and their team members. Everyone should understand their responsibilities and the standards by which success will be measured. This clarity prevents confusion and ensures that everyone is on the same page. Leaders need to demonstrate accountability through their actions. This means owning up to mistakes, following through on commitments, and taking responsibility for both successes and failures. When leaders model accountability, it sets the tone for the entire organization. Regular feedback is essential to holding leaders and team members accountable. Leaders should create an environment where constructive feedback is encouraged and seen as an opportunity for growth. This practice allows for continuous improvement and ensures that issues are addressed before they escalate.

Effective leaders promote open lines of communication where team members feel comfortable voicing concerns, offering suggestions, and giving honest feedback. Open communication helps leaders stay informed and ensures that they are aware of any challenges or issues that need to be addressed. Establishing regular check-ins and performance reviews helps maintain accountability. These meetings provide opportunities to assess progress, address challenges, and adjust goals, as necessary. They also create a space for leaders and their teams to reflect on successes and areas for improvement. Accountability must be a two-way street. Leaders should hold themselves to the same standards as their team members. This demonstrates fairness and ensures that accountability is seen as a shared responsibility rather than a top-down directive. Recognizing and rewarding accountability can encourage this behavior across the organization. Whether through praise, promotions, or other incentives, leaders should celebrate those who consistently take ownership of their work and demonstrate accountability.

Mistakes and failures are inevitable, but accountable leaders use these experiences as learning opportunities. They embrace challenges and setbacks as moments to reflect, grow, and improve. Encouraging this mindset helps create a culture where accountability is linked to personal and professional development. Accountability is essential for effective leadership because it strengthens trust, drives performance, and ensures transparency. By practicing accountability, leaders foster a culture where responsibility is shared and valued, leading to more ethical, transparent, and successful organizations. Leaders who embrace accountability create an environment that fosters growth, learning, and continuous improvement for themselves and their teams.

CONNECTING LEADERSHIP, EMOTIONAL INTELLIGENCE, AND SPIRITUAL INTELLIGENCE

Leadership, emotional intelligence, and spiritual intelligence collectively shape an individual's effectiveness as a leader. In today's complex and fast-paced world, it is essential for leaders to not only possess technical expertise but also emotional, spiritual, and interpersonal skills to engage and motivate others. The synergy of emotional intelligence (EI) and spirituality carries a profound impact on individual work success. Wayne Matthews and other researchers have correlated spirituality and high EI with the practice of interpersonal oriented leadership styles like the transformational leadership style.

Emotional intelligence revolves around recognizing, understanding, and managing both one's own emotions and those of others. Emotionally intelligent leaders build strong relationships, communicate effectively, and navigate difficult situations with empathy. They grasp the impact of their emotions on others and use this insight to create a positive work environment. In simpler terms, EI is the art of perceiving and comprehending one's emotions and those of others, enabling better decision-making and the creation of a harmonious work environment. High EI individuals often excel in leadership roles, as they are adept at detecting and diffusing potentially volatile situations. They foster effective communication and harmony within their teams.

Spiritual intelligence (SI), on the other hand, involves understanding one's own spirituality and connection to a higher power, whether through religion, belief in a greater force, or a sense of purpose. It helps leaders find meaning in their work, lead with integrity and compassion, and cultivate inner peace and balance. Susan Tee and her colleagues describe spiritual intelligence as a "set of abilities that individuals use to apply, manifest, and embody spiritual resources, values, and qualities in ways that enhance their daily functioning and well-being."

The combination of spiritual intelligence (SI) and emotional intelligence (EI) helps a leader create a positive work environment, boosting productivity and efficiency. According to Tee et al., spiritual understanding helps individuals recognize the root causes of behavior without judgment and address the genuine needs of others. Leaders with strong EI and SI gain a unique advantage, deepening their connection with employees on a meaningful level.

Leaders with high spiritual intelligence (SI) are likely to excel in interpersonal skills, aligning closely with an interpersonal-oriented leadership style. Emotional intelligence (EI), widely recognized as a key predictor of positive job performance, is a common trait among many highly successful business leaders. Together, leadership, EI, and SI create a powerful synergy. Leaders who cultivate these qualities develop an inspiring and effective leadership style that promotes the well-being of everyone involved, ultimately contributing to a better world.

NAVIGATING ATHEISM, SPIRITUALITY, AND LEADERSHIP

The landscape of leadership is a tapestry woven from various threads of beliefs, perspectives, and ideologies. In the intersection of atheism, spirituality, and leadership, a complex and intriguing dialogue emerges, challenging traditional notions and inviting a nuanced understanding of what it means to lead. Atheism, the absence of belief in a higher power or deity, often stands in contrast to spirituality, which encompasses a broad range of beliefs and practices that explore the transcendent or non-material aspects of existence. However, these concepts are not always diametrically opposed. Atheism can coexist with a profound sense of spirituality that revolves around interconnectedness, wonder, and awe for the universe's mysteries. In the realm of leadership, the traditional image of a charismatic, faith-driven leader has often been upheld. Yet, a growing cohort of leaders demonstrates that ethical, effective leadership is not contingent upon religious belief. Instead, it emerges from a deeper understanding of human nature, empathy, and the capacity to inspire and empower others.

Atheist and spiritual leaders alike often draw their ethical framework from diverse sources—philosophy, humanism, scientific principles, or spiritual philosophies rooted in mindfulness and compassion. They find common ground in fostering a culture of inclusiveness, ethics, and integrity within their organizations. Navigating diverse belief systems within a team or community can be both a challenge and an opportunity for growth. Effective leaders in this sphere embrace diversity, fostering an environment where differing beliefs are respected and contribute to a rich tapestry of perspectives that fuel innovation and creativity. Leadership in the intersection of atheism and spirituality often involves transcending the limitations of rigid ideologies. It demands a willingness to engage in dialogue, to learn from diverse perspectives, and to remain open to the possibility of personal transformation through understanding others' viewpoints.

Spiritual exploration, whether rooted in atheism or spirituality, often involves introspection, self-awareness, and personal growth. Leaders who traverse this intersection prioritize continuous self-improvement, understanding that personal growth enhances their leadership abilities and fosters a culture of growth within their organizations. Leadership at this intersection revolves around inspiring a sense of purpose that transcends individual beliefs. Whether through a commitment to social justice, environmental sustainability, or human welfare, these leaders ignite a collective sense of purpose that goes beyond religious or non-religious affiliations.

In the evolving landscape of leadership, the intersection of atheism, spirituality, and leadership presents a mosaic of possibilities. Embracing diversity, fostering ethical frameworks, and transcending boundaries become keystones for leaders navigating this complex terrain. It's not the absence or presence of belief that defines effective leadership, but the ability to inspire, empower, and unite toward a common, meaningful purpose. As the boundaries between belief systems blur, leaders who navigate this intersection with grace and wisdom pave the way for a more inclusive and harmonious future.

◆ ◆ ◆

CHAPTER FOUR

Psychological Theories and Spiritual Leadership

Throughout history, human beings have shown an inherent inclination toward worship, rooted in a universal belief in higher powers, transcendent forces, or divine entities. This phenomenon, documented across all cultures and epochs, underscores the ubiquity of spiritual belief. This shared aspect of human existence prompts significant questions about its influence on human behavior and decision-making. Understanding this deep-seated attraction to worship can shed light on how leaders think, act, and make decisions, particularly when influenced by their spiritual beliefs.

Historically, humans have organized themselves into groups for survival, with a leader naturally emerging in each group. Notably, some of history's most prominent figures have not only led but also founded major spiritual traditions and religions - such as Jesus in Christianity and Mohammed in Islam, among others. While spirituality is often examined through historical, cultural, or theological perspectives, and leadership analyzed in business and management contexts, the psychological connection between these two realms remains largely unexplored. This book aims to bridge that gap, offering a research-driven examination of how spirituality influences leadership, and exploring how these forces shape both individual leaders and broader societal dynamics.

Psychological theories, including Festinger's (1962) cognitive dissonance, Tajfel's (1982) social identity theory, and Maslow's hierarchy of needs, suggest that spirituality plays a pivotal role in human behavior and, consequently, leadership style. Maslow's theory underscores the insatiable nature of human needs and the drive for self-actualization, a pursuit commonly identified with leadership roles. It also posits that individuals seeking self-actualization often attain it by exploring the transcendent through spirituality. This idea is complemented by the concept that spiritual awareness is intrinsically linked to self-actualization, which may bridge the gap between one's ideal and actual behavior, as elucidated by Higgins' self-discrepancy theory. Furthermore, an individual's consciousness is a potent driver of behavior, signifying that leaders who espouse spirituality are inclined to act with purpose and intentionality, guided by their belief and values. Yasuno's research confirms the influence of heightened states of consciousness on neurological systems, indicating the profound impact of spirituality on human psychology.

The quest for love, peace, and harmony is a universal spiritual journey and foundational to most religions. The individual's need for esteem deeply influences behavior, as various psychological theories, such as Festinger's social comparison theory, Bem's social perception theory, Higgins' self-discrepancy theory, and Silvia and Duval's self-awareness theory, posit. Elevated self-esteem correlates with increased happiness and well-being, while a decrease in self-esteem is often linked to conditions such as depression and anxiety, as supported by Sharma and Agarwala. Spirituality and self-esteem are interconnected, both offering solace and coping mechanisms for those grappling with stress and psychological distress. Notably, individuals from marginalized groups, such as Black Americans in the U.S., have been reported to have elevated self-esteem because of focusing on their positive qualities to uplift their self-esteem, a phenomenon elucidated by Schroeder. This elevated self-esteem among Black Americans may be an inherited survival trait, passed down through generations. Similarly, spirituality, an intrinsic aspect of self, may be associated with coping and survival, leading to observable behaviors that align with both the self and spirituality.

COGNITIVE DISSONANCE AND SPIRITUAL LEADERSHIP: ALIGNING BELIEF AND BEHAVIOR

Leon Festinger's cognitive dissonance theory offers profound insights into the human experience, particularly when examining the intersection of spirituality and leadership. This theory posits that when individuals confront inconsistencies between their beliefs and actions, they experience a disconcerting emotional state. To alleviate this dissonance, people often adjust their attitudes to harmonize with their behavior. This book explores the profound implications of cognitive dissonance theory for organizational leaders who identify as spiritual. It explores how these leaders may grapple with aligning their spiritual beliefs with their leadership roles, and the consequences of failing to do so.

AN OVERVIEW OF COGNITIVE DISSONANCE THEORY

Festinger's theory suggests that when people experience a mismatch between their beliefs and behaviors, they feel emotional discomfort. If this discomfort persists, it can negatively impact mental health, potentially leading to issues such as stress, anxiety, and depression, which may, in turn, contribute to other physical health problems like high blood pressure, insomnia, weight issues, sexual dysfunction, some forms of addiction, and more. These effects of dissonance compel them to act in ways that diminish the perceived disharmony between their beliefs and behaviors.

In the context of leadership, this theory suggests that when an organizational leader's spiritual convictions conflict with the policies and practices they must enforce, cognitive dissonance may manifest. However, forced compliance has its implications. Festinger's work, complemented by research from James Carlsmith, emphasizes the impact of forced compliance on cognitive dissonance. Their seminal experiment, involving monetary compensation for claiming enjoyment in a tedious task, revealed that individuals alter their private opinions to align with their publicly expressed views. The findings affirm that individuals adjust their behavior to alleviate cognitive dissonance. Applying this insight to spiritual leaders, we can anticipate that they may adapt their leadership style and communication to minimize emotional discomfort stemming from discord between their spirituality and organizational mandates.

Cognitive dissonance extends beyond the theoretical realm, manifesting in various real-life scenarios. For example, studies exploring academic dishonesty indicate that individuals who compromise their values by cheating may experience feelings of guilt or dissonance, especially if religiosity is a significant aspect of their identity. The need to minimize this dissonance can motivate people to align their actions with their deeply held beliefs and values. Based on this, one should expect that spiritual leaders, driven by their commitment to moral, ethical, or religious beliefs, would seek to integrate these values into their leadership roles. The dissonance created when organizational policies conflict with their spirituality can lead to feelings of guilt or shame. As a result, these leaders may reinforce commitment to their beliefs which then influences their leadership style.

Cognitive dissonance theory provides valuable insights into the complex relationship between spirituality and leadership because spiritual leaders sometimes find themselves at a crossroads, striving to harmonize their deeply rooted beliefs with their roles in organizations. By recognizing the emotional impact of cognitive dissonance, leaders can gain a deeper understanding of their challenges and take measures to align their spirituality with their leadership. This approach promotes more authentic and ethically grounded leadership practices.

Cognitive dissonance's influence is closely tied to the self, which continually strives to enhance its self-esteem and align with its social identity. This means that human beings are psychologically wired to naturally behave or act in ways that elevate their self-esteem and connect them to their in-group or other things or beliefs they identify with. This suggests that leaders who personally or socially identify as spiritual are intrinsically driven to balance their self-concept, the core of their spirituality, with their organizational role. The dynamic interaction between these components influences how they lead, make decisions, and navigate ethical dilemmas.

KEY CONCEPTS OF SOCIAL IDENTITY THEORY

Social Identity Theory, initially conceptualized by Henri Tajfel, provides valuable insights into human behavior, group dynamics, and leadership practices. It posits that individuals strive to boost their self-esteem by adjusting their behavior to favor the social groups with which they closely identify. This phenomenon leads to the preference for in-group members, or those who share commonalities in intergroup situations. The subconscious manifestation of this behavior can take the form of social dominance orientation, potentially resulting in discriminatory practices when left unchecked.

Social dominance, as outlined in the social identity theory, is evident in various global divisions and conflicts rooted in ethnicity, politics, and religion. Historical instances, like World War II and the Rwandan genocide, highlight this phenomenon. Similarly, the Christian crusades spanning the 11th to the 16th century and the Islamic revolution and movements led by groups like Al Qaeda in the early 2000s, exhibit terrorism and manifestations of social dominance. This trend extends into politics, where extremist factions resort to violence driven by an unwavering desire for their affiliated group or party to gain or remain in power at any cost. This trend intensified notably in the United States following President Biden's election, culminating in the extreme actions witnessed during the attack on the United States Capital on January 6, 2021. However, this example is not exclusive to the US, a specific political party, or any specific group; it is a prevalent phenomenon in democracies worldwide.

LEADERSHIP AND SPIRITUAL ALIGNMENT

The application of social identity theory to leadership offers valuable insights into how some leaders align their organizational management with their faith, religion, or spiritual beliefs. For example, Chick-fil-A's CEO publicly supported traditional marriage, citing his religious convictions and belief in the biblical definition of marriage as being between a man and a woman. His statements generated significant controversy, eliciting both support and backlash from various groups. Additionally, Chick-fil-A's policy of closing on Sundays, established by its founder S. Truett Cathy, reflects his desire to provide employees with a day for rest, family time, and worship, rooted in his Christian faith. These examples underscore the significant influence of a leader's spiritual identity on their management practices.

Like Chick-fil-A, Cadbury was also influenced by the spirituality of its founders. The founder of Cadbury, John Cadbury, was a Quaker, and his spirituality deeply influenced the company's structure, culture, and treatment of employees. Quaker beliefs emphasize equality, integrity, and social justice, which shaped Cadbury's business practices. Quakers were known for their commitment to honesty and fair dealing. This ethos was ingrained in Cadbury's business operations, promoting fair trade and quality products. The company avoided products like alcohol and tobacco, which Quakers found morally objectionable, and focused on producing wholesome goods, like chocolate, which aligned with their values.

Cadbury's spiritual values also led to a strong emphasis on

the well-being of employees. John Cadbury and his successors implemented progressive labor practices for the time. They introduced shorter work hours, fair wages, and safe working conditions, which were uncommon during the industrial era. The Cadbury brothers built the Bournville village in the late 19th century, a model community that provided workers with comfortable housing, recreational facilities, schools, and healthcare services. This initiative was grounded in the Quaker belief in nurturing both the physical and moral well-being of individuals, aligning with the universal principle of the golden rule found in many religions.

Cadbury's Quaker background also fostered a sense of community within the company. The firm promoted a culture of respect and mutual support among its workers, encouraging a sense of belonging. This approach created a collaborative and inclusive environment, which not only improved employee morale but also boosted productivity and loyalty to the company. The Cadbury family was involved in various social reform efforts, including campaigns against poverty and support for education. They believed that businesses had a responsibility to contribute to the greater good, reflecting the Quaker principle of stewardship. This philosophy of social responsibility continued to influence Cadbury's corporate policies long after the founder's era. John Cadbury's spirituality, rooted in Quaker principles, shaped the company into a pioneering force for ethical business, employee welfare, and social progress. This legacy of integrating spiritual values with business operations set a standard for socially responsible corporate behavior. The company also engaged in various philanthropic activities, including supporting education and healthcare initiatives which laid the groundwork for what we now recognize as corporate social responsibility

SOCIAL IDENTITY THEORY, LEADERSHIP, AND THE GOLDEN RULE

Research based on Social Identity Theory has explored how spirituality, peer pressure, and culture influence decision-making. It suggests a strong connection between spirituality and transformational leadership - a leadership style focused on prioritizing others' needs. Transformational leaders often embody the principle of the Golden Rule: treating others as they wish to be treated. This universal moral guideline is shared across various cultures and religions, expressed differently but emphasizing empathy, kindness, and fairness.

In Christianity, the Golden Rule appears in Matthew 7:12: "Do unto others as you would have them do unto you," and in Galatians 5:14: "For the entire law is fulfilled in keeping this one command: 'Love your neighbor as yourself.'" Other faiths and philosophies echo similar teachings:

• Islam: "And be good to others as Allah has been good to you." (Quran 28:77)

• Hinduism: "Refrain from inflicting upon others such injury as would appear undesirable to us if inflicted upon ourselves." (Yogahastra 2:20)

• Taoism: "Regard your neighbor's gain as your own gain; regard your neighbor's loss as your own loss." (T'ai Shang Kan Ying P'ien)

• Buddhism: "Hurt not others with that which pains yourself." (Udana Varga 5:18)

This alignment explains why transformational leaders often display spiritual inclinations and prioritize their employees' needs in decision-making. It highlights the natural harmony between personal beliefs and effective leadership, where compassion and fairness guide actions.

Michael Hogg's Social Identity Theory of leadership proposes that prototypical leaders, exemplifying behaviors, and opinions congruent with organizational norms, are perceived as charismatic, efficient, and effective. In contrast, leaders deviating from these norms may encounter challenges. Organizations typically favor leaders who align with established behavioral norms, which may necessitate behavioral adaptation for atypical leaders. This conformity to organizational norms can introduce dissonance and hinder the performance of inherently capable leaders.

Workplace spirituality, intergroup relationships, and sense-making are deeply connected to social identity.

Leaders often identify not only with their organization but also with smaller groups within it, such as work teams, age cohorts, or informal lunch groups. Social identification frequently forms shared traits like ethnicity, spirituality, or age, highlighting the importance of group unity in shaping social identity. This also shows how reducing out-groups can strengthen connections and foster a cohesive environment.

Understanding the role of social identity in leadership is essential. Leaders may unintentionally favor their in-groups, a form of implicit bias, which can leave those outside these groups feeling excluded. Effective leaders actively address this bias by creating structures that promote inclusivity, while less effective leaders may remain unaware of their biases or dismiss their significance. Social Identity Theory helps in understanding leadership, organizational culture, and group dynamics. Leaders must balance personal values, spirituality, and leadership carefully. To promote effective leadership and minimize implicit bias, both leaders and organizations should be aware of social identity theory principles and their impact on workplace diversity.

THE INTERPLAY OF COGNITIVE DISSONANCE
AND SOCIAL IDENTITY

Cognitive dissonance arises when individuals hold inconsistent beliefs, values, or behaviors. To alleviate this discomfort, they may adapt, justify, or alter these conflicting elements. Social identity, on the other hand, encompasses the self-concept derived from one's affiliation with social groups, such as race, ethnicity, religion, gender, or political inclination, and the convergence of these two psychological phenomena has been extensively explored within the realm of social psychology.

Research revealed that cognitive dissonance is closely intertwined with social identity. People often employ their social identity to mitigate cognitive dissonance by selectively processing information that aligns with their existing beliefs and values. This mechanism, known as identity-protective cognition, safeguards self-esteem and sustains a positive self-image by avoiding information that challenges one's social identity. An illustrative instance is "biased assimilation," where individuals gravitate toward information that reaffirms their preexisting convictions and disregard contradictory data. This selective processing is particularly pronounced in matters closely linked to one's social identity, such as political beliefs, religion, or social attitudes. Individuals who strongly identify with specific groups are more likely to experience cognitive dissonance when confronted with conflicting information, prompting engagement in identity-protective cognition.

Social identity pressure and cognitive dissonance synergistically contribute to biased assimilation, a cognitive bias where people interpret new information in a way that reinforces their existing beliefs and attitudes. This bias led individuals to place more value on evidence that supports their current views while disregarding or minimizing evidence that contradicts them. For example, someone with strong political or religious beliefs is likely to view information that aligns with their ideology as more credible, dismissing data that challenges it. This dynamic often results in more polarized views and an increased resistance to changing one's stance, even when faced with compelling contradictory evidence, as seen in religious and political discussions.

Another example of biased assimilation is evident in vaccine hesitancy fueled by misinformation from social media or other sources. Despite substantial scientific evidence supporting vaccine effectiveness, some individuals resist vaccination, aligning themselves with social groups that oppose it. During the COVID-19 pandemic, patterns of resistance led to higher rates of hospitalizations and fatalities, highlighting the influence of group identity and social pressures over factual evidence. In gang culture, biased assimilation caused by cognitive dissonance and social identity pressures are likewise evident. Gang members, influenced by loyalty to their group and the cognitive dissonance effect of acting against it, may engage in criminal activity that leads to crime, violence, and incarceration, demonstrating how social identity can drive some people to make decisions that are against their self-interest and preservation, or life-threatening and life-changing choices.

In leadership, biased assimilation can lead leaders to make decisions based on their personal beliefs, spirituality, or group affiliations, which may unintentionally alienate some employees. To address this, many organizations implement Diversity, Equity, and Inclusion (DEI) programs or adopt policies like setting quotas for minorities in leadership roles or on company boards. However, some individuals or groups oppose DEI efforts, seeing biased assimilation as a way to benefit their personal or groups' interests.

This bias tendency is also visible in U.S. politics. Democratic presidents often advocate for social services and liberal policies, while Republican presidents focus on conservative values and fiscal discipline. Even institutions like the judiciary, which are expected to be neutral, show signs of biased assimilation.

For instance, the U.S. Supreme Court's decisions, such as overturning Roe v. Wade with a conservative majority or legalizing same-sex marriage with a liberal majority, illustrate how deeply held beliefs can shape outcomes, even in spaces meant to be impartial.

Social identity also exerts influence via social comparison. Individuals frequently assess their beliefs and behaviors by contrasting them with those of their reference groups. In this situation, the presence of dissonance arises when discrepancies emerge between one's convictions and those of the reference group. Strongly identifying with a particular group intensifies cognitive dissonance when countering beliefs or behaviors conflict with those of the group. In response, individuals may opt for identity-protective cognition or realignment of their beliefs with those of the reference group to maintain self-consistency.

Social comparison can help explain why ordinary people may lean toward political extremism or why those without religious beliefs may become radicalized. This idea also applies to leaders, influencing how they make decisions. Leaders often base their decisions on their social identity, which includes their political, cultural, and religious views. They tend to compare themselves and their choices to peers in their field, often copying the actions of similar businesses. For example, some leaders who initially supported full-time remote work during and after the COVID-19 pandemic later reversed their stance, mostly because other companies in their industry made the same change, without relying on solid data or reasons for their shift.

IMPACT OF SOCIAL IDENTITY ON BEHAVIOR

Understanding how spirituality influences leadership becomes increasingly crucial due to research indicating that individuals often rationalize their actions when these align with their social identity, even if these actions stray from ethical norms or contradict personal beliefs. For instance, leaders deeply connected to a religious group may justify ethically questionable behavior if it aligns with their group's values.

In many countries, politicians advocating for an abortion ban based on religious beliefs exemplify this. Similarly, in numerous countries, homosexuality remains illegal due to religious and cultural beliefs. In some extreme cases, publicly identifying as a gay person is a capital offense, as evidenced by an Iranian man's execution in January 2019 for engaging in gay sex. However, one may argue that what one considers as ethical may be subjective based on personal belief and culture, which ultimately determines what one perceives as right or wrong because of biased assimilation. When these individuals hold positions of power, their decisions can have a significant impact on the lives of others, including life-and-death consequences.

COGNITIVE DISSONANCE, SOCIAL IDENTITY, SPIRITUALITY, AND LEADERSHIP

Cognitive dissonance, social identity, spirituality, and leadership are intricately linked concepts that possess the potential to profoundly influence an individual's thoughts and behaviors. Cognitive dissonance represents the discomfort experienced when one holds contradictory beliefs, values, or behaviors. This mental tug-of-war prompts individuals to seek resolution by either adapting their beliefs and behaviors or actively pursuing new information to harmonize the discord. Social identity involves how individuals define themselves in the context of social groups, be it related to race, ethnicity, gender, religion, or nationality. Social identity has the power to shape beliefs, values, and behaviors, and, conversely, is molded by individuals' perceptions of how their group is viewed by others. Spirituality is yet another intricate thread woven into this tapestry, influencing cognitive dissonance and social identity. For many, spirituality serves as a guiding light, helping individuals reconcile conflicts between their beliefs, values, and behaviors. It can also sculpt one's sense of self and the connection to others, thus molding their social identity and how they experience cognitive dissonance. Leadership serves as the overarching process of influencing others to achieve a shared goal or objective. Leaders encountering cognitive dissonance or conflicts between their beliefs, values, and behaviors may find effective leadership challenging. These inner contradictions can erode their credibility and effectiveness as leaders. However, leaders who skillfully navigate and resolve cognitive dissonance, aligning their thoughts and actions with their convictions, tend to lead with authenticity and integrity.

In essence, cognitive dissonance, social identity, spirituality, and leadership are complex and interwoven concepts that mold an individual's thoughts and behaviors. Understanding and skillfully managing these elements are pivotal for personal and professional growth and development. By acknowledging these interconnections, individuals can journey towards more authentic, effective, and inspiring leadership as demonstrated by the participants who were interviewed for this book.

THE RIPPLE EFFECT OF DISSONANCE ON PHYSICAL AND MENTAL WELLBEING

In the domain of human cognition, cognitive dissonance exerts a distinctive influence. This phenomenon emerges when individuals encounter conflicting beliefs, attitudes, or behaviors, engendering a state of psychological discomfort. While cognitive dissonance is commonly scrutinized within decision-making and behavior modification contexts, its repercussions for physical and mental health are equally profound. Therefore, comprehending the ramifications of cognitive dissonance on both physiological and psychological aspects of health elucidates its extensive reach because persistent dissonance has been reported to negatively impact mental health, potentially leading to issues such as stress, anxiety, and depression, which may, ultimately, contribute to other physical health problems like high blood pressure, insomnia, weight issues, sexual dysfunction, some forms of addiction, and more.

Cognitive dissonance significantly affects mental health by contributing to heightened levels of stress, anxiety, and emotional turmoil because when confronted with conflicting beliefs, individuals may grapple with uncertainty and doubt, fostering a persistent sense of unease. Research by Elliot Aronson and Judson Mills (1959) illustrates that individuals experiencing cognitive dissonance often employ coping mechanisms such as confirmation bias or avoidance to alleviate discomfort. Paradoxically, these strategies, while aimed at resolving dissonance, can perpetuate narrow-mindedness, exacerbating mental distress. Moreover, alterations in beliefs or actions to mitigate cognitive dissonance may disrupt one's sense of identity and stability, influencing decision-making processes adversely. Contrarily, cognitive dissonance may also contribute positively to mental health by fostering satisfaction or justification of one's choices, particularly irreversible ones. It can serve as a motivating factor for behavior change, such as engaging in physical activity after indulging in excessive eating while on a vacation or during the holiday season.

The impact of cognitive dissonance extends beyond mental health to influence physical wellbeing. Prolonged exposure to cognitive dissonance can induce chronic stress, leading to adverse physiological effects such as inflammation, cardiovascular issues, and compromised immune function. Studies have linked unresolved cognitive dissonance to an increased risk of hypertension, heart disease, and other stress-related ailments. Moreover, persistent mental strain from cognitive dissonance can disrupt sleep patterns, resulting in fatigue and impaired cognitive function.

Addressing cognitive dissonance for wellbeing necessitates recognizing its impact on both physiological and psychological fronts. Cultivating cognitive flexibility and critical thinking skills empowers individuals to navigate conflicting beliefs adeptly. Additionally, mindfulness practices like meditation foster heightened self-awareness and mitigate distress stemming from cognitive dissonance. Therapeutic interventions such as cognitive-behavioral therapy (CBT) target irrational beliefs, facilitating cognitive restructuring to alleviate associated discomfort.

The multifaceted impact of cognitive dissonance on physical and mental wellbeing underscores the imperative of addressing its effects comprehensively. By fostering awareness, critical thinking, and mindfulness, individuals can cultivate resilience in managing conflicting beliefs. Through targeted interventions and a holistic approach to wellbeing, efforts to mitigate the adverse effects of cognitive dissonance on health can be enhanced, empowering individuals to navigate life's complexities with greater self-awareness and resilience. Recognizing the significance of spirituality in potentially eliciting cognitive dissonance constitutes a critical initial measure in mitigating its impact on an organizational leader's emotional and physiological health.

◆ ◆ ◆

CHAPTER FIVE

Leading With Spirit: The Intersection of Spirituality and Leadership

This book examines how psychological concepts like social identity and cognitive dissonance shape leadership and decision-making. It draws insights from in-depth interviews with ten leaders who identify as spiritual. Through their personal stories, the leaders share details about their organizations, personalities, spiritual beliefs, and leadership styles. They reflect on their current roles and past experiences, showing how their spirituality guides their approach to leadership.

Characteristics of Study Participants

Participant	Job Title	Gender	Race/Ethnicity	Religion
Participant 1	Director	M	Black/African American	Christianity / Jehovah's Witness
Participant 2	Vice President	F	Asian/Pakistani	Sikhism
Participant 3	Regional Sales Manager	M	Caucasian/Jewish	Judaism
Participant 4	President	M	Hispanic/Mexican	Christianity / Pentecostal
Participant 5	Principal	M	Caucasian/ American	Christianity/ Catholic
Participant 6	Manager	F	Caucasian/ American	Christianity / Pentecostal
Participant 7	Director	F	Asian/Indian	Islam
Participant 8	General Manager	M	Black/African	Christianity / Pentecostal
Participant 9	Team Lead	M	Black/African	Christianity / Pentecostal
Participant 10	Supervisor	M	Black/African	Christianity / Pentecostal

Participant 1: A Portrait Of Spiritual Leadership

P articipant 1, a married African American man, and Director in his organization, emerges as a unique and compelling figure whose life and leadership are profoundly shaped by his spirituality. With three daughters and a son, and a junior college education as his highest attainment, he exemplifies a distinctive blend of personal values and professional dedication.

For Participant 1, spirituality is akin to unwavering trust in a divine creator, a profound belief in something larger than oneself. This faith directs his conduct, inspiring him to align his life with higher principles. He earnestly adheres to the teachings of Jehovah's Witness, a faith he embraced since the tender age of 5. His conviction is succinctly put: "Spirituality to me means to trust in the divine creator. Trust that there's something bigger than us. Knowing that the way I live my life is not solely something that I can dictate. I have to look to a higher being in terms of trying to live my life in harmony with His desires. So, spirituality... to me is believing... there is a creator, believing that He has a right to dictate how we should live our lives, and also believing that we should always be looking to please Him."

Participant 1 defined spirituality succinctly as "trust in the divine creator," which shaped his values of trust, honesty, and integrity. His goal was to live his life "in harmony" with God, extending these principles to his professional role. He prioritized honesty with his employees, keeping them "in the loop in terms of decisions and direction" to build trust. He believed that "telling the truth, being honest, and candid—even if it's unwelcome—is essential," as people handle the truth better when it's delivered sincerely. He also emphasized that his reliance on God guided him to remain honest in all situations, despite opportunities to act otherwise, stating, "If you trust in God, He will ensure you're cared for."

Participant 1 expected honesty and integrity from his employees as well. He encouraged open communication, assuring his team that truthful conversations would strengthen their partnership. "If you don't tell me the truth, I won't trust you, and we can't have a strong partnership," he explained. His compassion for employees was evident in his commitment to treat them "the way I want to be treated." He supported his staff by mentoring them, helping them grow professionally, and investing in their development, acknowledging that "to achieve the right way, you have to invest in people." Although he prioritized achieving organizational goals, he never lost sight of the importance of treating employees well. He humanized his role as a leader, emphasizing, "I'm not just a title; I'm a person just like you." He made decisions with consideration for their potential impact on employees, demonstrating compassion and sensitivity. He preferred to inspire commitment rather than impose authority, explaining that he sought employee buy-in by articulating the reasoning behind decisions.

Participant 1 described his decision-making process as guided by his spiritual values, always considering whether a choice would "honor or displease God." He placed God at the center of his priorities, maintaining that "it's always God first," followed by family, and then work. His leadership style was rooted in his conscience and moral values, which he described as "trustworthiness, dependability, truthfulness, respect, and high morals." By aligning his actions with these principles, he ensured that his conscience remained clear.

In addition, Participant 1 was people-focused, demonstrating "fellow feelings" for employees and mitigating the negative impacts of business decisions wherever possible. He described striking a balance in decision-making: "I can take care of the needs of the company but also make decisions that take care of the person as well." As one of the few Black leaders in his organization, Participant 1 saw his leadership role as an opportunity to advocate for diversity and equity. He sought to create a workplace environment where "everyone is treated equitably" and recognized his responsibility to "bring about a little bit more equality" and support employees from underrepresented backgrounds. He acknowledged the challenges of inequality he faced as a minority leader, explaining that he sometimes had to "conform to the environment" to maintain his position and open doors for others.

Participant 1's spirituality and leadership intertwined with his identity. He described himself as someone with a strong sense of self, noting that others might interpret his actions as personality or style rather than spirituality. Nevertheless, his behavior was an authentic reflection of his values and beliefs. His spirituality extended beyond personal belief, directly influencing his leadership approach. He operated with fairness, respect, and compassion, treating others as he wished to be treated—a reflection of the "golden rule." His focus on honesty and ethical decision-making helped build trust and fostered meaningful relationships with his employees. Despite his dedication to his role, Participant 1 maintained a clear perspective on corporate loyalty, stating, "There is no sense of loyalty from a corporation, but I love what I do." However, his priority remained with God and family, underscoring that spirituality and integrity were more important than material success.

In summary, Participant 1's spirituality was a compass that directed his personal and professional life. His leadership was characterized by honesty, compassion, and advocacy for equity and diversity. By aligning his actions with his core values, he ensured that his conscience remained clear and his leadership impactful. For him, spirituality was not just a belief but a way of life that shaped his decisions and relationships.

◆ ◆ ◆

Participant 2: Beacon Of Spiritual Leadership

Participant 2 is a 46-year-old married American woman of Pakistani descent, with two children—a son and a daughter. Holding a Master of Arts (MA) degree, she serves as Vice President of two non-profit organizations. As a practicing Sikh, her life and leadership are deeply rooted in her spirituality and the Sikh way of life. She describes herself as a people-focused, service-oriented, and democratic leader who draws inspiration from Guru Gobind Singh's egalitarian leadership model, which emphasizes equality and servant leadership.

For Participant 2, spirituality is a state of positive spirit, or 'Chardi Kala,' a mindset where one maintains a balanced state of mind regardless of circumstances. She said "... spiritual simply means staying in that state of mind of positive spirit or 'Chardi Kala.' It doesn't matter what happens - you are always in a balanced state of mind, and you accept things as they come, as the will of God." She stated further, "it's not complicated, you spend your days serving others, and ... being in that state of gratitude. That's our spirituality." It is the unwavering acceptance of life's events as the will of God.

To Participant 2, spirituality signifies maintaining a state of "Chardi Kala" - a positive and ascending state of mind. She explained, "You are always in a balanced state of mind, accepting things as the will of God." Spirituality for her involves gratitude, service to others, and embodying positivity. Her faith's teachings guide her to embrace challenges with grace and gratitude, finding peace and resilience through prayer, meditation, and service.

Participant 2 integrates her spirituality into daily practices, including prayer and exercise. Sikh prayers, she noted, are poetic and musical, enabling her to stay physically, emotionally, and mentally healthy. She shared how spirituality helps her cope with stress: "When I have a stressful situation, a poetic hymn will come to mind... reminding me not to feel anxiety." For her, staying active and reflective embodies the Sikh holistic approach to health, which encompasses physical, emotional, and spiritual well-being.

Participant 2's leadership philosophy is rooted in serving others. She sees herself as a facilitator rather than an authoritarian leader: "It's not me telling you what to do," she said, preferring to guide through collaboration and empowerment. Her faith inspires her to value creativity and critical thinking over rigid adherence to uniform solutions. "The end goal is important, but what's more beautiful is how people think while they're trying to reach it," she remarked, highlighting her emphasis on process over product. She believes in creating an equal playing field for her employees and models this approach after Sikh Gurus who championed gender equality and justice. She actively stands against unfair practices, often confronting higher authorities with courage rooted in her spirituality. When facing conflict, she seeks peaceful resolutions but is ready to defend fairness and justice, embodying the dual qualities of the Sikh "saint-soldier." As she explained, "You become a soldier to defend equality and justice—not just for yourself but for any defenseless person."

Participant 2's Sikh faith profoundly influences her confidence and resilience. She described her spirituality as a source of inner strength, enabling her to navigate workplace challenges without fear: "My spirituality gives me confidence. I don't focus on saying what's perceived as 'right.' I say what I want to say." Her strong sense of justice and self-awareness stems from her faith, allowing her to reject practices that conflict with her principles.

As a leader, she prioritizes compassion and service, treating her role as an extension of her faith. "When I'm teaching students, it's a form of service," she said, underscoring her commitment to serving others. Her interpersonal leadership style emphasizes understanding others' perspectives and resolving conflicts amicably, while remaining firm in her principles.

A central aspect of Participant 2's identity is the Sikh doctrine of the "saint-soldier." She described this as balancing peacefulness with the readiness to protect and defend others. "The saintly characteristic comes before the soldier trait," she noted. This balance is evident in her leadership, where she is both compassionate and assertive, standing up for her team and advocating for fairness. Her spirituality also fosters optimism and positivity. She believes that serving others and practicing gratitude are key to maintaining a joyful and balanced life. "A Sikh is always in a state of optimism," she said, describing "Chardi Kala" as her guiding principle. She works to cultivate this optimism in her team, building trust and accountability while leading with empathy.

While Participant 2 identifies as Punjabi by culture, she draws a clear distinction between cultural traditions and her Sikh faith. She rejects aspects of Punjabi traditions that conflict with her spiritual values. Her gender identity also shapes her leadership experience. She shared challenges she faced as a woman leader, navigating biases from those unaccustomed to women in decision-making roles. Her spirituality empowers her to confront these biases confidently.

Participant 2 integrates spirituality into every facet of her life. From prayer and meditation to service and leadership, her faith provides her with a framework for self-reflection, stress management, and personal growth. "Search your own heart daily, and you'll never feel stress or anxiety again," she advised. Her spirituality keeps her balanced, resilient, and committed to living with purpose.

Participant 2's spirituality is a core part of her identity, influencing her leadership style and overall approach to life. She embodies the qualities of a "saint-soldier," combining compassion, courage, and optimism in her interactions with others. This translates to a leadership style characterized by integrity and a deep commitment to serving others. She consistently strives to align her actions with the principles of the golden rule, treating others with the same respect and kindness she would expect to receive.

◆ ◆ ◆

Participant 3: A Guided Leader Of Integrity

Participant 3, a 57-year-old married Jewish man with two sons, serves as a Regional Sales Manager, and his profound spirituality shapes every facet of his life and leadership. He wants to be identified as a "mensch," a Yiddish term for someone with integrity, honor, and strong character—essentially, a decent and responsible person. For him, spirituality transcends the mundane and elevates humans above mere animals. It is the pursuit of wisdom, knowledge, and ethical conduct, distinguishing us from the primal focus on survival. He said, "spirituality means something that elevates us above animals. Animals... wake up and the only thought is, where is my next meal coming from... for us it's trying to acquire wisdom, trying to acquire knowledge, in addition to... where our next meal is. According to him, spirituality is "an instruction for life." In Participant 3's view, spirituality acts as a guide for life, shaping how he interacts with friends, family, and colleagues. It encompasses both personal feelings and organized religion, providing a sense of peace, ethical boundaries, and an overall feeling of well-being. Judaism is not just a religion but a life guide, offering wisdom about the essentials of existence.

"If you think about the Ten Commandments, it should be like a foundation to everything."

For this participant, spirituality served as a guide for living - a framework that influenced his interactions with friends, family, business associates, and ethical decision-making. He described spirituality as encompassing a broad spectrum, from feelings and approaches to life to organized religion. His faith in Judaism, which he considered a "life guide" and source of wisdom, shaped his approach to leadership, relationships, and personal growth. He emphasized the importance of setting aside time to nurture spirituality, stating, "We can't all build our own houses, grow our own food, sow our own clothes; there will be no time for spirituality." He likened spirituality to a fundamental human need, comparing it to water and food as essential for a meaningful life.

Participant 3's spirituality significantly influenced his leadership style, which was rooted in ethical principles and people-focused practices. He viewed his role as a leader as one of service and support, working collaboratively with his team to achieve shared goals. He strived to inspire his employees by offering guidance and modeling the behavior he expected, saying, "I don't ask them to do something that I wouldn't do." He extended to his employees the mentorship he had received earlier in his career, reflecting a commitment to their development and success. His faith dictated his behavior in the workplace, where he treated others with respect and compassion, aligning his actions with the golden rule: "Treat your neighbor like you want to be treated." He believed in the importance of perspective-taking, especially when dealing with difficult individuals, saying, "I try to put myself in their shoes... and try to come to a solution."

Participant 3 avoided gossip and was mindful of his words, understanding the potential harm of careless remarks. He emphasized ethical interactions, noting, "I try to think of a way that is straight, is correct, is ethical." His spirituality also fostered inclusivity and respect for other faiths. He valued respectful interactions with people of different religions, stating, "I feel very comfortable and close to people who are religious... as long as we are all respectful of each other's religion." Family was central to his values, and he adhered to the principle of equality, believing that "God says to us... treat everyone equal." Gratitude was a cornerstone of his spiritual practice, and he expressed deep appreciation to God for both small and significant blessings. He felt dissonance and guilt when he failed to show gratitude or strayed from his spiritual practices, such as neglecting prayer or Sabbath observance. To atone for his sins, he regularly prayed and sought forgiveness. He described spirituality as a source of balance and inner peace, saying, "It puts me at ease, at peace... and just feeling good." Participant 3 saw his faith as a lifelong journey of learning, continually exploring the depths of Jewish teachings to deepen his spirituality.

In summary, Participant 3's spirituality deeply influenced his leadership style, interactions, and personal conduct. His people-centered leadership was guided by ethical principles derived from his faith, including respect, compassion, and fairness. He sought to align his actions with his spiritual values to avoid guilt and maintain a clear conscience. For him, spirituality was not only a guide but also a source of strength and fulfillment in both his personal and professional life. He described spirituality as a source of balance and inner peace, saying, "It puts me at ease, at peace... and just feeling good."

◆ ◆ ◆

Participant 4: A Faith Driven Leader

Participant 4 is a 50-year-old American man of Hispanic descent who has been married for 22 years with two children. He holds a college degree and serves as the president of a financial organization. While raised as a Catholic, he later embraced Pentecostal Christianity. His deep-rooted faith in Christ and spirituality permeates his personal and professional life. Participant 4 firmly believes in emulating Christ's teachings, recognizing that the Christian faith calls its followers to mirror the life and values of Christ. He doesn't see this as a gray area; it is a clear and unambiguous directive. He said, "When I pay close attention to my faith, when I pay close attention to the Christian faith, to the teachings of Christ, we are called to be like Him, this is not a grey area, we are called to be like him."

Compassion was the foundation of the interpersonal-oriented leadership style described by Participant 4. His spirituality deeply influenced his leadership approach, decision-making, sense of identity, compassion, prayer habits, obedience, ethics, and role modeling. Unlike many, this participant did not grow up deeply spiritually but became more so with age. He reflected, "I was never really moved by faith growing up... I didn't understand much about Christianity. Our faith grew in church, so we became more faithful. We attend church now, and I definitely consider myself a Christian." For him, spirituality was tied to selflessness, stating, "As a Christian, you have to put yourself second in many cases... and I believe how you treat others is very important." His approach to others was rooted in treating people with "dignity, compassion, and care." This selflessness, he noted, brought personal fulfillment: "Put yourself second even for a moment, and you realize how much better you feel... the Holy Spirit likes when you put someone else first."

Participant 4's spirituality shaped how he treated his employees and customers. He emphasized paying employees fairly and encouraging work-life balance: "I encourage them to take time for their family. I encourage them to treat our customers with kindness and compassion, not because it will get us more business, but because it's the right thing to do." He extended compassion to customers, particularly those in need. For instance, "We waive our fees for professions like teachers, veterans, and first responders because they do so much for the community." The biblical Golden Rule guided his decisions: "I treat everybody the way I want to be treated... with dignity and respect." This people-focused leadership style reflected his belief that "ethics and harmony make for more sound decisions in the long run." His spirituality influenced his decision-making process, especially in business. He avoided focusing solely on profits, instead building an organization equally committed to employee rights, community support, and creating a harmonious environment: "We're no longer just worried about making a dollar... I want a workplace where stress is low, harmony prevails, and the focus is on the right things."

He often prayed before major decisions, including hiring: "Values I'm developing as a Christian spill into my business... I could increase profit by compromising ethics, but I refuse to do that." This commitment extended to ensuring fairness and rejecting greed: "If there's a dollar that doesn't belong to me, I don't want it ... I want Caesar's to go to Caesar, and I want God's to go to God." Obedience to God was central to Participant 4's spirituality. He stated, "God doesn't need my attention, love, or money—He wants my obedience." This obedience extended to his work: "Taking my faith and putting it to practice at work is part of being obedient." He viewed salvation as the ultimate reward for this obedience, emphasizing, "It's about exchanging your sin for salvation, and in return, you become obedient to God." Fear of consequences for disobedience motivated him: "There are consequences to people's actions... in the long run, we are judged by our acts of obedience to God."

Participant 4 strived to emulate Christ in his leadership. "If I want people to see Christ, the best way is for me to act and be like Christ... treating people with compassion, avoiding judgment, and leading by example." His leadership style prioritized kindness, fairness, and a focus on others' well-being. He highlighted the importance of leading with integrity: "This is not a grey area; we are called to be like Him. I am being called to act like He did." His goal was to ensure that others saw the "fruit of God" in his actions, regardless of faith or denomination.

Participant 4's spirituality shaped his personal and professional identity. He described feeling content and free from greed, saying, "I don't need more, I don't want more... I'm not money hungry." His spirituality brought him satisfaction and shaped how he cared for his physical and emotional well-being. His interpersonal focus extended to fostering a positive organizational culture. "We are an organization equally interested in making money, protecting employee rights, and creating harmony." He emphasized that leadership rooted in spirituality requires putting others first: "The Holy Spirit rewards selflessness."

Participant 4's spirituality was integral to his leadership style. It guided his interactions, decision-making, and organizational culture. His faith inspired compassion, fairness, and obedience, driving him to align his actions with biblical principles. For him, being a leader meant "treating people with dignity, compassion, and care" and avoiding sin through ethical behavior and obedience to God. Spirituality was not just a personal belief but a transformative influence that shaped his leadership and life.

◆ ◆ ◆

Participant 5: A Spiritual Leader Guided By Faith

Participant 5 is a 35-year-old Caucasian American man with three children, a master's degree, and certification in school leadership. He proudly serves as the principal of a Catholic high school, deeply committed to his Christian faith. In his own words, "Spirituality for me, in a nutshell, is how we communicate with the transcendent, that which is greater than us." Participant 5's journey into leadership is guided by a profound spirituality that extends its influence into every facet of his life. Spirituality is not an abstract concept but an active force shaping his leadership style, decision-making, and relationships. He embraces a people-centered approach to leadership, prioritizing the well-being and emotions of individuals over mere tasks. He believes in the importance of harmony and the quality of relationships, reflecting, "I definitely value how people are feeling and how they are doing over necessarily the task at hand." His leadership is marked by a pastoral and compassionate demeanor, and he strives to help people become the best versions of themselves.

Spirituality is the compass guiding his leadership style and decision-making. He frequently turns to his faith and spirituality for guidance when faced with difficult choices, entrusting them to God. For him, every decision is rooted in discernment, "Is this the choice I think God wants me to make?" His spirituality transcends his personal life, shaping his professional decision-making. He seeks this divine guidance through prayer, and he continually considers the impact of his decisions on the individuals involved. Participant 5 places great trust in his employees, an attitude nurtured by his spirituality.

The principle of putting God first serves as a foundational principle for Participant 5. His spirituality is the heart of his leadership and profoundly impacts how he interacts with others, the approach he takes to his work, and the allocation of his time. He believes that being a Christian provides him with a sense of peace and purpose, helping him understand his gifts and talents while challenging him to use them for the greater good. Prayer plays an essential role in his life, centering him and offering solace. He seeks consolation and connection with God through prayer, using it as a tool to balance his emotions and prepare himself for the challenges ahead.

Participant 5 has a strong belief in sin and forgiveness, acknowledging his own flaws and the need for continuous self-improvement. He understands the significance of forgiveness, both from God and toward others, as a path to salvation and transformation. His compassion knows no bounds. He models himself after Jesus, seeing every individual as created by God and deserving of love and dignity, regardless of differences. Even in the face of disagreements or hurt, he seeks love, understanding that this is the spiritual path he must follow. Throughout his life and leadership, gratitude is another vital component of Participant 5's spirituality. He begins and ends his days in prayer, offering thanks to God.

His leadership style and decision-making were deeply rooted in his spirituality. "We are encouraged to tie our spirituality in with our leadership and decision-making; that's part of our character," he explained. While he valued understanding others' perspectives, saying, "I like to be informed of what others think or feel when making a decision," he ultimately turned to God for guidance in challenging situations. "When discernment becomes really difficult, you put it before God: which choice will better serve and glorify Him in the decision?" he shared. His faith was the cornerstone of his decision-making process. "The root of all my decisions when it comes to discernment is: is this the choice I believe God wants me to make? And that's hard —it takes a lot of faith on my part." His spirituality extended beyond his personal life, influencing his professional decisions as well. "I can't separate my faith from my decision-making," he admitted. Prayer played a vital role in his process: "I pray in my office, asking God for guidance, questioning Him on what my next decision or step should be." He also deeply cared about the well-being of his employees, always mindful of how his choices would affect individuals. "I'm always concerned about how my decision impacts the person it affects," he emphasized.

Participant 5's spirituality shaped his leadership style, fostering trust and empowerment among his employees. "I think that involves spirituality—you have to have faith and trust in others, care for people, and still hold them accountable," he explained. He preferred to lead from behind the scenes, describing himself as "a servant" and striving to avoid "the God-complex." Instead, he aspired to be seen as a servant leader, saying, "I want to smell like my sheep," meaning he was deeply involved in the work of those he supervised. "I do everything that's asked of the people I supervise," he shared, adding, "I model the behavior I want to see in them."

For Participant 5, God was always at the center. "It's not about me; it's about God and God's desire and will. I'm okay when it's not about me." His spirituality was "the heart of how I lead," shaping his interactions, approach to work, and even how he managed his time. He described spirituality as "how we communicate with the transcendent, that which is greater than us."

As a Christian, his faith was inseparable from his identity. "I can't separate that from who I am," he said. His faith brought him peace, calm, and comfort, giving him a profound sense of connection with God. "Being a Christian helps me understand who I am and recognize my gifts and talents. At the same time, it challenges me daily to use those gifts and talents for the greater good," he reflected.

Participant 5's spirituality profoundly influenced his leadership, identity, and relationships. He described prayer as a central practice, saying, "Prayer centers me, makes me feel peaceful and calm, giving me a feeling of consolation." While most of his prayer experiences were comforting, he acknowledged that, at times, "prayer leads me into more distress or stress," but these instances were rare.

Participant 5's leadership style was deeply people centered. "I like to think I have a good sense of how people are feeling. I hate to see people dejected, angry, or frustrated." His decision-making reflected a focus on individuals, as he often weighed how decisions would affect those impacted. He consistently tied his leadership to his spirituality, modeling his actions after Jesus, whom he considered "the ultimate model for me." He sought to emulate Jesus' humility and servant leadership, explaining, "I try to do everything that's asked of the people that I supervise. I model the behavior that I want to see out of them." His leadership reflected a deep sense of humility: "Humility keeps me grounded, helping me to see others as equals and to avoid any impression of being superior or authoritarian." As a servant leader, he prioritized the well-being of others, saying, "I'm always going to try to do what's in the best interest of our faculty and staff, benefactors, and ultimately, God—doing what God wants." He believed in accountability but balanced it with compassion, explaining, "I care for people while holding them accountable."

Central to Participant 5's spirituality was the belief that "everyone has an inherent human dignity, regardless of culture, race, religion, or sexuality." This perspective informed his approach to relationships and leadership. "When I look at a person, I see someone I believe was created by God, so I try to be loving towards everyone," he shared. His spirituality enabled him to show compassion even in difficult situations. "I think my spirituality leads me to love people no matter what, even those who disagree with or are angry at me. I still care for those people." Forgiveness was also a cornerstone of his approach: "My spirituality guides me to love, even if I feel betrayed or disappointed." He aspired to love as God loves, reflecting, "God loves Satan as much as God loves Mary and Jesus. God is constant, outpouring love and grace. While I can't attain it, I do my best to try to love like God loves." His ultimate goal was "to love at all costs" and to act in a way that reflected divine love. "I think love is the most spiritual way to act," he concluded.

Participant 5 saw his faith as inseparable from his identity and decision-making. "Being Christian...I can't separate that from who I am," he explained. Prayer was foundational to his sense of self and daily life: "I begin and end the day in prayer. Prayer centers me, prepares me for what's coming, and gets me in the right mindset." He described deeply moving spiritual experiences that shaped his identity. "Those experiences of God are essential to who I am. If I'm not living that out, I'd want to know how I can better live it in my life." His spirituality gave him a sense of peace and purpose, helping him understand his gifts and challenging him to use them for the greater good.

In his relationships, he cherished harmony and celebrated the successes of others, saying, "I take more pleasure in other people's accomplishments than my own." He viewed relationships as sacred and treated them with respect and care. "You recognize that relationship is a sacred thing, and there is something sacred about being together and trying to care for one another."

In summary, Participant 5 was a Christian leader whose faith influenced his identity, leadership, and relationships. He based his decisions and growth on spirituality, aspiring to embody humility, love, and compassion like Jesus. "My spirituality is the heart of how I lead; it's the very center of how I interact with others," he explained. For Participant 5, being identified as a spiritual leader who reflected God's love and values was essential to his sense of self.

❖ ❖ ❖

Participant 6: A Life Guided By Faith And Compassion

Participant 6 is a remarkable 70-year-old Caucasian American widower who, during her 47-year marriage, became a proud parent to three stepchildren, a grandparent to 14, and a great-grandparent to 13. Her educational journey concluded with a high school diploma, but her life's path took her on a profound spiritual journey from Catholicism to Pentecostal Christianity. Beyond her spiritual life, she was also a successful high-end retail store owner. In her own words, "It (spirituality) encompasses your whole life; it sifts through you and whatever you do, and whatever you think, and whatever you say.

The role of spirituality in Participant 6's leadership style was expressed through spiritual guidance, decision-making, leadership approach, prayer, faith, obedience, salvation, compassion, role modeling, trust, spiritual identity, ethical values, and her relationships with others. She derived much of her leadership philosophy from her Christian faith, emphasizing the Bible as a foundational guide. She stated, "I pray to Him before I make any decisions…I constantly ask the good Lord for wisdom, guidance, and direction every day, and for Him to guide my steps." Her leadership was predominantly people-oriented, focusing on the needs of others. She believed spirituality should permeate all aspects of life: "It's not only going to church—that's a dead end. It must come out of the church, seep from your head to your heart, and be reflected in every decision you make… it's a sifter of good and bad and predicates all of your decisions."

Prayer and obedience to God were central to her life and

leadership. She followed the Pentecostal Christian doctrine and emphasized salvation as the ultimate goal: "I keep my eyes on heaven... when you die, you have nothing left, nothing." She modeled her life on the Bible verse Matthew 6:33: "Seek ye first the kingdom of God and His righteousness, and all other things will be added unto you." Obedience to God's will was non-negotiable for her: "If you really love the Lord, then you are obedient." This belief influenced her business practices, such as closing her store on Sundays, even during peak seasons, to honor the Sabbath. For her, obedience was part of a spiritual battle: "To be obedient to God's will is a difference between good and evil." She viewed God's commandments as a protective guide and stated, "I obey the Ten Commandments because you know that's a hedge of protection."

Faith played a significant role in her life, as she explained, "Faith is the key that opens the door to all of God's riches and blessings." She prioritized her relationship with God over her business, saying, "My business is on the sideline now—God is my real job." She trusted God to provide for her needs, declaring, "When I take care of God's business, He is going to take care of my business."

Participant 6 was compassionate in her relationships and modeled her behavior after Christ. She described herself as "kinder, gentler, and thoughtful" toward her employees, respecting them as individuals and acting as a role model by exemplifying Christian values. She stated, "I try to behave in a godly way" and aimed to be "a good example of what a Christian is." Her leadership style evolved as her spirituality deepened. She noted, "I used to, a long time ago, fly off the handle at my employees." I don't do that anymore." Instead, she demonstrated patience, offering support and comfort, such as sharing Psalm 23 with those in distress. She strived to emulate Christ, saying, "I model my behavior to be more Christ-like, the way He was when He was here for 33 years."

Her relationship with God was deeply personal and trusting. She described God as her "husband, best friend, and savior." This trust grew through her experiences of God's faithfulness, as she stated, "I can look back and see how faithful He's been... and why is He going to stop now?"

Ethical principles rooted in her spirituality guided her business practices. She maintained honesty, explaining, "We keep clean books... we don't have cash under the table." She believed in consistency between her faith and actions, saying, "You don't have one foot in the world and one foot in God. You act the same way whether you're in church or at the mall."

In summary, spirituality was the foundation of Participant 6's leadership style, decision-making, and relationships. Her faith informed every aspect of her life, from business ethics to interpersonal interactions. Her people-centered leadership emphasized compassion, respect, and modeling Christ-like behavior. Guided by prayer, obedience, and trust in God, she viewed her role as both a leader and a servant, striving to reflect her spiritual values in all she did. Her Christian faith was not just a belief system but a comprehensive framework that shaped her identity, actions, and leadership philosophy.

◆ ◆ ◆

Participant 7: Navigating Leadership Through Faith And Compassion

Participant 7 is a 65-year-old American woman of Asian Indian descent who is happily married with two adult sons. Holding a master's degree and serving as a director within an organization, she draws her strength and guidance from her Muslim faith. Her perspective on spirituality is profoundly insightful, as she states, "Spirituality is seeking meaningful connection with someone who is much more superior than you."

Participant 7 described her leadership style as deeply rooted in spirituality, which guided her decisions, relationships, and overall approach to leadership. She emphasized her reliance on spiritual principles such as prayer, faith, obedience, compassion, and accountability. Her leadership was influenced by her belief in divine guidance, stating, "You can't be a leader without the belief that there is a higher authority... You're just a puppet." She saw herself as a servant-leader, embodying the principle: "I will serve you and then I will lead you."

Her decision-making relied on prayer and seeking Allah's guidance. For critical decisions, she performed "Istikhara" prayers, noting, "When hiring people, I don't sign a contract till I have prayed for about a week." This spiritual reliance extended to her daily life, as she prayed for fairness and justice in her work and sought blessings from Allah for success. She believed her leadership was ultimately accountable to Allah, saying, "Whatever you do, you have to do it for the pleasure of your creator."

Participant 7 was interpersonally oriented, emphasizing relationships over tasks. She avoided being authoritarian, asserting that "people are important, not projects... if I win over people, projects will automatically be successful." Her approach to subordinates was one of mentorship and friendship, stating, "I'm coming in to identify your strengths and to make you stronger... I'm just a friend." She modeled exemplary behavior explaining, "Whatever I preach, I must practice." Her interactions reflected compassion, trust, and a focus on uplifting others. The Quran and the prophet Muhammad were her moral and leadership compass. She viewed the Quran as "a way of life" that informed all aspects of her existence, striving to follow the prophet's example: "We always pray that Allah guides us to walk in the footsteps of the prophet." This inspiration underpinned her servant-leadership style, as she believed, "A leader is the servant of the people, so I can't just sit down, boss around."

Forgiveness was central to her leadership and personal well-being. She valued the act of forgiving others as a spiritual practice, saying, "Allah says to forgive... it softens your heart." Her ability to forgive and seek forgiveness helped alleviate guilt and brought her peace, enabling her to "look at myself in the mirror and say I'm not guilty of anything." She extended this philosophy to others by helping them grow and improve. Material wealth did not motivate her; instead, she prioritized spiritual rewards and giving back to others. "Monetary reward is not something I look for... I've never looked for monetary gains," she explained, emphasizing her desire to volunteer for the sake of Allah.

Her spirituality shaped her ethical standards, which guided her decisions and actions. She was committed to doing what was right, despite challenges, and sought strength through prayer to make ethical choices. A self-described workaholic, she strove for excellence in all areas of her work, viewing her organization as an extension of her family. "Like for your family, you would do anything... This is my second family," she remarked. Participant 7's relationship with Allah brought her gratitude, humility, and a sense of purpose. Through prayer, she expressed her thankfulness for the blessings in her life, often becoming emotional when reflecting on them. "The blessings that I have received are immense... it humbles you," she shared. Her spiritual practices, including daily prayers and supplications, reinforced her connection to Allah and her commitment to living a life aligned with Islamic values.

In summary, spirituality was the cornerstone of Participant 7's leadership. Her Islamic beliefs shaped her identity, guided her decisions, and influenced her compassionate, servant-oriented approach to leading others. She lived and led with humility, accountability, and a deep sense of purpose, continually striving to align her actions with her faith and to serve as a role model.

◆ ◆ ◆

Participant 8: A Spiritual Guide In Leadership

Participant 8, a 65-year-old African American gentleman, has been happily married for 33 years and is a father of three children. With a Ph.D. in engineering, he stands as the Founder and General Manager of his own company. His spiritual journey began as a nominal Christian before experiencing a profound transformation as a "born-again" Pentecostal Christian. Not only is he a leader within the Pentecostal Church, but he's also an influential figure in the business world.

To him, spirituality is a profound force that governs human existence. He asserts, "Spirituality makes us cautious of the kind of life we live because we believe that there will be consequences for everything that a man does... ultimately. Spirituality also leads us to believe that there is life after death, and man is accountable to either eternal damnation or eternal acceptance into the kingdom of God."

Participant 8 highlighted the profound role of spirituality in shaping his leadership style, particularly through elements such as faith, blessings, consequences, spiritual experiences, spiritual connection, ethics, compassion, trust, role modeling, spiritual guidance, and decision-making.

He believed that all events in the physical world originated from the spiritual realm, asserting that spirituality provided him with extraordinary abilities. He described feeling empowered by God's presence, stating, "Being a spiritual person, I feel like I'm not alone. I feel that I have other powers that I can bring to use when I need to do something." His leadership style was people-focused, requiring adaptability and interpersonal skills: "When you are people-focused...you have to change your style." Guided by his Christian faith, he sought direction from the Holy Spirit, particularly in ethical decision-making. "The Holy Spirit is...the conscience before you do anything that is evil; he will prompt you, 'Oh, that's not right.'"

Participant 8 modeled his leadership and decision-making after Jesus Christ, emphasizing the importance of asking, "What would Christ do in this kind of situation?" His interactions with others reflected this spiritual framework. He demonstrated trust in God to care for his needs, believing that "God will not give me a cross that is too heavy for me to bear." Compassion and fairness were central to his relationships with employees, whom he treated like family: "I don't just treat them like employees; I treat them as my relations, and in so doing, I am able to get the best of their services." He likened his organization to a church, where empathy and understanding were paramount: "If a staff member is not feeling too good or is going through some challenges, we put aside the work he has to do in the interim and empathize with him."

Integrity, fairness, and respect were core principles of his leadership. He endeavored to lead by example, showing qualities such as kindness, generosity, and empathy. "They see in you a kind of person they love to be...Those are Christian principles, but you don't have to label them as such to demonstrate them." He also emphasized the importance of role modeling in appearance, speech, and conduct: "Role modeling includes your appearance, your manner of speech, and your ability to relate to people in decent jokes."

Participant 8's spirituality profoundly transformed him after converting to Pentecostal Christianity. He abandoned a previous "law of the jungle" mindset for a focus on personal relationships with Christ. He viewed spirituality as both a motivation and deterrent against unethical behaviors, stating, "When you experience the real change that makes you now a Christian with a relationship with Christ, you can't operate in those things again because your conscience will not allow you." His conscience, which he identified as the Holy Spirit, played a central role in his personal and professional identity.

He believed his life and actions were under divine control, describing himself as being led by "an unforeseen force that we ascribe to God Almighty." This conviction guided him to avoid sin and embrace the belief in rewards and consequences, both in this life and the hereafter. "There is a God that's looking at you... He controls your destiny, and He can terminate it at any second." His awareness of eternal accountability motivated him to align his behavior with his spiritual beliefs.

Spirituality also shaped his leadership philosophy and decision-making processes. By partnering with Christ in his business, he ensured that his actions and choices aligned with Christian values. "When you want to make any decision, however critical, you ask yourself, 'What would Christ do in this situation?'" His reliance on the Holy Spirit served as a moral compass, prompting him to act ethically and responsibly.

Participant 8's spirituality inspired him to treat his employees with empathy, build strong interpersonal relationships, and model ethical behavior. He believed in living by the golden rule, "You do as you'll be done by," and prioritized compassion and fairness in his leadership. His interpersonal-oriented leadership style reflected his spiritual values and belief in fostering a supportive, family-like environment at work.

Ultimately, Participant 8's life and leadership were deeply influenced by his spirituality, which provided motivation, guidance, and a moral framework. His belief in divine accountability, the importance of compassion, and the power of role modeling underscored his commitment to leading with integrity and faith. This commitment extended to all aspects of his life, aligning his leadership style with his spiritual convictions and values.

❖ ❖ ❖

Participant 9: A Guiding Light Of Spirituality In Leadership

Participant 9, a 46-year-old African American man, and father, brings a wealth of experience and spirituality to his role as a Registered Nurse and team leader, holding a graduate degree. His journey is one of transformation, evolving from his Catholic upbringing to becoming a "born-again Christian" and ultimately the Head of a Pentecostal Church.

For Participant 9, spirituality isn't just a concept; it's the essence of one's immortal being, a connection to the divine source. He eloquently explains, "Spirituality is the aspect of your being that is immortal, that does not die... your spirituality is a connection to the one that made you, because God is a spirit, so he put His spirit in us, and we became a living soul... spirituality is having a relationship with the one whom we all came from, and that is God who is the spirit." Spirituality played a central role in shaping Participant 9's leadership style, influencing his approach to decision-making, spiritual guidance, prayer, forgiveness, interpersonal relationships, faith, and ethical conduct. His leadership philosophy was deeply rooted in his identity as a Pentecostal Christian, shaped by a transformative spiritual experience.

Participant 9 identified as an interpersonal-oriented leader, describing his approach as compassionate and supportive. "So, I am not ... job-oriented... I will help you; I will empathize with you," he explained. His leadership involved "carrying people along" and providing employees with the necessary support to succeed. For example, he emphasized being emotionally and mentally present for his team: "If they need materials, resources, help, whatever it is that they need, I like to be there mentally, emotionally for them and give them whatever they need to get their job done." This relational approach reflected his emphasis on empathy and care for others.

Prayer played a pivotal role in Participant 9's decision-making process. He sought divine guidance for both professional and personal decisions, often praying before acting. "You pray, and ... then you call the people and say, 'This is what the Lord is saying, and ... this is where the Lord is leading us,'" he shared. Despite his deep faith, Participant 9 respected diverse beliefs in the workplace. While he openly lived out his faith, he refrained from imposing it on others, saying, "You don't have to force somebody to come...to accept Jesus Christ." He experienced a profound transformation after converting from Catholicism to Pentecostal Christianity. He described moving from being "religious" without a personal relationship with God to developing a deeper connection with Him. "I have been religious but not having a relationship with the Lord...very religious in going to church but not having a relationship with my God who is a spirit," he said. This transformation brought him spiritual enlightenment and a sense of renewal: "Once you align your will to the will of God, there will be this excitement... like you're intoxicated!" This spiritual awakening reshaped his values, leading him to avoid sin and seek forgiveness through prayer. He described prayer as his "lifeline" and a solution to all challenges: "Prayer is everything. Prayer ... brought me here ... You solve problems by praying! You go to pray!!" His trust in prayer reflected his belief in its mysterious and transformative power.

Participant 9's spirituality influenced his ethical decision-making at work. He followed organizational policies unless they conflicted with his faith, asserting, "I cannot go to work and commit sin and come back to God." His actions were guided by a commitment to righteousness and his belief that "If a man is right with God...everything will fall into place." In addition, his spiritual transformation led him to avoid behaviors that could lead to guilt or dissonance. When he felt he had sinned, he sought forgiveness through prayer, saying, "I was wrong, Lord, please forgive me."

Participant 9's spirituality shaped his interactions with colleagues and subordinates. He treated others with care, compassion, and fairness, regardless of their beliefs or backgrounds. "Everybody keep their belief outside, and we do the work, whether you're gay, whether you are straight, whether you are atheists, whether you are agnostics," he explained. This inclusive approach reflected his respect for individual differences while maintaining his spiritual convictions. His relationship with God also informed his trust in divine provision and guidance. He believed that obedience to God's will ensure success and stability: "If a man is right with God... everything will fall into place."

For Participant 9, spirituality was inseparable from his leadership style and daily life. He emphasized that spirituality "involves everything we do in the church, in our family, in our own lives, at work, in our secular job, even at play, and social gatherings." His trust in God and reliance on prayer shaped his decisions, relationships, and leadership practices, ensuring alignment with his faith.

In summary, Participant 9's spirituality served as a guiding force in his leadership, influencing his compassion, decision-making, and commitment to ethical behavior. His belief in prayer as a lifeline and his dedication to living a life aligned with his faith exemplified his spiritual foundation in all aspects of his personal and professional life.

◆ ◆ ◆

Participant 10: A Guiding Light
Of Spiritual Leadership

Participant 10, a 49-year-old African American man, father, and leader, brings a unique blend of experiences to his roles. With a background in engineering, service in the U.S. military and the city police department, and his pastoral duties at a Pentecostal Church, his life is a testament to a transformative journey. Having grown up in a secular environment, Participant 10's spiritual awakening occurred as an adult when he became a "born-again Christian." His faith serves as a guiding force in his leadership style, leaving an indelible mark on how he interacts with others, models compassion, and makes decisions. He asserts, "Being spiritual, especially if your own spirituality teaches you love, compassion, and how to be selfless and help others, there is no way you won't be a better leader."

Participant 10's leadership style was deeply influenced by his spirituality, which guided his decisions, interactions, and ethical framework. His faith shaped his interpersonal-oriented approach, characterized by compassion, role modeling, and a strong sense of spiritual and moral accountability. He identified as an interpersonal-oriented leader, prioritizing the welfare of others over strict adherence to job performance. He explained, "Honestly, I've found some situations whereby I was more concerned about somebody's welfare than whether the person is doing the job." His leadership approach was grounded in his belief in a "higher code of operation than the code that the company gave," emphasizing obedience to God's will over workplace policies. He expressed confidence that pleasing God would ensure excellence in his professional duties: "If I'm pleasing God, there's no way I will not be able to please my employer."

This conviction was a source of motivation for him to exceed expectations, driven by his faith rather than material rewards: "There are other things that actually push me to do my best rather than even the company... and that is my own faith." He sought guidance from the Holy Spirit in decision-making, trusting that it would remind him of applicable principles from his faith: "The Holy Spirit will just help you make that decision... this is what you're supposed to do." Prayer was central to Participant 10's spirituality and daily life. He developed the habit of praying regularly, even briefly, to seek guidance and support: "It may just be a few seconds of prayer... something came to your mind, you need help, God, I need help on this." He also prayed preemptively to avoid challenges that might later compel him to seek divine intervention, saying, "You pray so that you don't have to pray."

Participant 10's belief in life after death and God's omnipresence shaped his sense of accountability and quest for salvation. He prioritized earning God's approval over professional recognition, emphasizing, "God is the highest judge who can judge my actions... eternal destiny is more than what any job can offer." He followed his faith's teachings to avoid actions that could jeopardize his salvation, relying on obedience to God and trust in His judgment. He experienced emotional discomfort, or dissonance, when workplace policies conflicted with his spiritual beliefs or negatively impacted others. For instance, as a police officer issuing tickets, he said, "I didn't really enjoy it... I did it, but that's not the way I thought I was going to enjoy it." In such cases, he prioritized his spirituality, declaring, "If there's any real direct contradiction, I will choose the higher code."

Participant 10's spirituality shaped his interactions with others, inspiring compassion, and fairness. He believed in showing care for his employees' welfare, stating, "My compassionate part always comes in, especially if I know this individual has always been doing their best." He trusted that such compassion would be reciprocated, adding, "When they know that you are concerned, they will be able to even give you their best, even when you're not watching them." He extended compassion even in corrective actions, emphasizing the need to "apply [policies] with a human face" rather than rigidly. He reflected, "We are the human face that the policy needs." As a police officer, he kept a personal set of jumper cables in the trunk of his patrol car to assist people with dead batteries, even though it wasn't part of his official duties. His desire to help others brought him fulfillment: "I felt much better when I do something to help somebody." However, he experienced internal conflict when unable to show compassion due to policy constraints, saying, "The time that I feel worse... is when I can't help somebody."

Participant 10's compassion was rooted in his Christian belief, including the golden rule: "God says you should love your neighbor as yourself... treating somebody else the way you like to be treated." This belief drove him to treat others equitably and supportively, even bending backward to assist those of different faiths, guided by his faith's emphasis on tolerance: "Tolerance! Tolerance!!" He influenced others by modeling behavior consistent with his faith, stating, "My behavior is doing the preaching." He treated all employees equally and fairly, demonstrating his commitment to inclusivity and justice. Despite this, he acknowledged the necessity of balancing compassion with judgment, as he modeled his actions after God: "God... loves, but God... also judges." He believed in maintaining a clear conscience in leadership, stating, "When you have conscience, when you are leading people, you don't want to do things that will affect people negatively." This principle ensured that his decisions aligned with his spirituality and sense of fairness, fostering peace within himself: "I have peace within me that I'm making the right decision, even if somebody else hates it."

Participant 10 described a profound spiritual transformation after becoming born again. He explained that this change eradicated desires for sin and vices: "When I became born again... there were certain desires that stopped... when I became born again that desire just ended." This transformation brought him peace and joy: "Peace of mind that surpasses all human understanding... joy cannot really be explained; it is better experienced than explained." His spirituality gave him confidence in eternal life and motivated him to live in obedience to God's teachings: "We are saved by grace through faith... however, even when God saves us through Jesus Christ, there are... expectations... like our way of life, our conduct."

Participant 10's leadership reflected his spirituality in decision-making, compassion, and concern for others' welfare. He described an instance as a police officer where he prioritized humanity over strict adherence to the law, by providing assistance to a stranded woman: "If we applied the letter of the law, we could have left her on the street... but we demonstrated a little bit of the human side." His focus on spiritual accountability, ethical leadership, and interpersonal care made him a leader who modeled fairness, compassion, and a commitment to moral principles. He prioritized obedience to God and aligned his leadership style with his Christian faith, demonstrating the role of spirituality in shaping his decisions and relationships.

◆ ◆ ◆

The Essence Of Spirituality And Religion In Leadership

An analysis of all ten participants revealed that spirituality significantly influenced their adoption of an interpersonal-oriented leadership style. Through interviews, these participants emphasized how spirituality shaped their approach to leadership, with a consistent focus on compassion and concern for others, such as employees, teammates, and subordinates. This approach was underpinned by the "golden rule," often summarized as treating others as one would like to be treated. One participant articulated this principle by referencing God's teaching: "Love your neighbor as yourself, that's treating somebody else the way you like to be treated."

Spirituality also guided these leaders' decision-making at work. Many participants noted that their ethical and harmonious choices were rooted in spiritual values rather than pragmatic or financial considerations. For example, one leader reflected: "If you're making pragmatic decisions just based on the financial side of things... it's a slippery slope. But if you focus on ethics and harmony, it's a more sound decision." Prayer played a central role in decision-making, as these leaders sought divine guidance. One participant described praying Istikhara for critical decisions, while another explained, "Prayer is part of decision-making. That's where we pray 'the examine.'" Many believed that God or the Holy Spirit, through prayer, provided clarity during challenging moments.

Some participants saw their obedience to spiritual principles as bringing rewards and blessings. One said, "The blessings that I have received are immense. As I drive, I start counting what I'm blessed with." Conversely, fear of sin and its consequences shaped their actions. One participant remarked, "Whatever a man does, he has to pay the penalty," underscoring their awareness of ethical accountability.

The participants often experienced inner conflict or guilt when acting against their spiritual beliefs. This dissonance motivated them to align their behaviors with the dogma of their faith or religion. One leader described this feeling: "You can do something, and nobody sees, but where is your conscience? How do you feel about yourself?" As a result, they consistently aimed to make decisions that preserved peace of mind and harmony, even at a financial cost.

The leaders exhibited strong ethical values derived from their spirituality. Traits such as fairness, integrity, loyalty, dependability, and respect were frequently highlighted. One participant elaborated: "When you and I have a contract, there must be fairness, integrity, and dutifulness regardless of what's happening." Gratitude and forgiveness were also integral to their spirituality. Leaders expressed daily gratitude to God and sought forgiveness both from God and others. One stated, "I believe in forgiving and forgetting. I may not forget, but I'm willing to forgive and move on."

These participants' spirituality influenced their relationships, performance, and overall leadership style. They identified as people-oriented leaders, with one noting: "Honestly, I've found situations where I was more concerned about someone's welfare than whether they were doing the job." Their spirituality also fostered learning and self-improvement. One leader explained, "My religion has so much depth that I'm always learning. It's a lifetime job."

Respect and equitable treatment of employees were central to their leadership approach, reflecting their spiritual principles. One participant shared: "Because of my religion, I treat my colleagues and those who report to me with respect." Prayer and meditation were common practices, with leaders using them for guidance, gratitude, and decision-making. As one described: "All decisions—business, personal, financial—are precipitated by prayer."

The leaders' trust in God was unwavering. One expressed it as: "If I take care of the Lord's business, He is going to take care of my business." Obedience to God was also a recurring theme. As one participant put it: "God wants my obedience. Because He wants it, I'm going to give it to Him."

These leaders modeled the behaviors they wanted to see in others, often guided by religious teachings or figures such as Jesus, Mohammed, Moses, or the Sikh Gurus. One explained, "We are called to be like Him... I'm being called to act like Him [Jesus]. It's about being a role model." Another noted: "The prophet Mohammed said a leader is the servant of the people, so I can't just sit down and boss around."

Sin, forgiveness, and salvation were critical motivators for their obedience to spiritual principles. One leader summarized this: "That's what salvation is about—exchanging sin for salvation and becoming obedient to God."

All participants aligned their leadership styles, ethical values, and decisions with their spirituality, describing it as inseparable from their identity. "Being Christian, I can't separate that from who I am," one leader shared. They reported unique spiritual experiences, such as feelings of peace, joy, and calmness, which positively influenced their leadership. One participant described spirituality as: "It keeps me happy, confident, and calm. Internally, you're just a calm person."

Despite their diverse religious affiliations, these leaders demonstrated remarkably similar spiritual influences on their leadership. They prioritized ethical behavior, compassion, and interpersonal connections. Spiritual practices such as prayer, meditation, and gratitude shaped their decision-making and reinforced their values. Overall, their spirituality deeply influenced their leadership style and interactions, grounding them in the values of fairness, respect, trust, and a steadfast commitment to the golden rule: treating others as they would wish to be treated.

◆ ◆ ◆

CHAPTER SIX

Qualities of Faith-Based Leadership

This book explored human qualities, psychological theories, lived experiences, and personal ethical values linked to effective leadership. Based on their lived experiences that were shared through interviews, these leaders highlighted a range of traits and values, including: blessings, calmness, consequences, decision-making, dissonance, equality, fairness, faith, forgiveness, honesty, gratitude, leadership style, learning, loyalty, meditation, obedience, optimism, peace, positivity, prayer, relationships, respect, role-modeling, salvation, self-identity, spiritual connection, spiritual experience, spiritual guidance, spiritual identity, and trust. These qualities and personal character traits demonstrate how the golden rule, spirituality, religion, and leadership are interconnected, as shown in figure 2.

Spirituality

- Calmness
- Dissonance
- Equality
- Meditation
- Peace
- Spiritual connection
- Spiritual identity
- Spiritual experience
- Spiritual guidance

Golden rule

Religion

-Blessing
- Consequences
- Fairness
- Faith
- Forgiveness
-Honesty
- Gratefulness
- Obedience
- Prayer
- Salvation
- Self identity

Leadership

- Decision-making
- Leadership style
- Learning
- Optimism
- Loyalty
- Positivity
- Relationship with others
- Respect
- Role modeling
- Trust

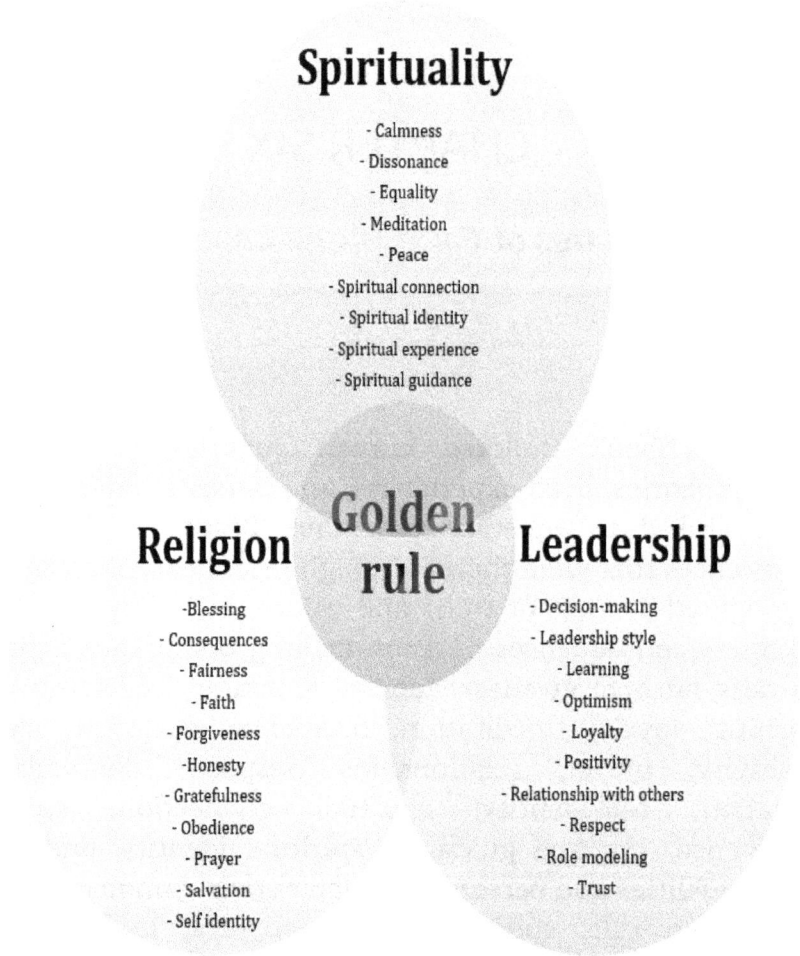

Figure 2: Qualities of Faith Led Spiritual Leadership

Remarkably, many of these qualities are in harmony with the teachings of various religious scriptures, transcending the boundaries of individual faiths. For instance, in the Christian tradition, the Bible speaks of the fruit of the Spirit, encompassing love, joy, peace, patience, kindness, goodness, faithfulness, gentleness, and self-control (Galatians 5:22-23) which resonates with the values expressed by interviewed.

These leadership qualities are not limited to Christianity but are rooted in the universal values found across various religions and their sacred texts. The Quran, the Torah, and many other religious writings emphasize attributes like compassion, justice, humility, and faithfulness—values that align closely with those identified by the leaders interviewed for this study.

As a result, the characteristics of effective leadership derived from these interviews transcend individual religious traditions. They reflect universal principles that can guide leaders of diverse spiritual backgrounds. Whether a leader identifies with Christianity, Islam, Judaism, or another faith—or even holds a more secular worldview—they can find inspiration in these shared ethical values and traits.

By adopting these principles, leaders can strengthen their decision-making, build meaningful relationships, and create positive changes in their businesses, organizations, and communities. In the sections that follow, we will take a closer look at each of these qualities and explore how the interviewed leaders described their significance and application in real-world leadership.

1. Blessing

Both spiritual blessings and good leadership are grounded in the concept of connecting with a higher power, whether through religious faith, a belief in a higher purpose, or a sense of profound meaning in life. When these two concepts intersect, they create a potent force for positive change. Spiritual blessings are the divine gifts that individuals receive because of their connection to a higher power. These blessings manifest in various forms, such as inner peace, a deeper understanding of one's purpose and values, or the ability to navigate life's challenges with grace and resilience. They provide the strength and support needed to lead with integrity and compassion, making them a priceless resource for leaders.

Good leadership, conversely, revolves around making a positive impact on the world through effective decision-making and guiding others toward common goals. Leaders who are recipients of spiritual blessings possess the tools to lead with purpose, align their decisions with their values and beliefs, foster workplaces founded on compassion and empathy, and navigate the trials of leadership with poise and resilience. In practical terms, the synergy between spiritual blessings and good leadership can manifest in numerous ways. Leaders who incorporate spiritual practices into their daily routines, like meditation or prayer, can remain connected to their values and beliefs. As a result, they make decisions grounded in their profound spirituality. These leaders are also primed to create work environments characterized by compassion and empathy while navigating the challenges of leadership with grace.

The deep connection between blessings and leadership is not exclusive to any particular faith. Various religious traditions and their scriptures emphasize the importance of blessings and the rewards of good deeds. This universal perspective on blessings ties into the leaders' motivations to perform acts of kindness and goodness, driven by a desire to receive divine blessings. In the Bible, Deuteronomy (15) declares, "The Lord thy God shall bless thee in all thou doest". The Quran (16:53) similarly acknowledges blessings, stating, "Whatever good thing you enjoy, it is from God." The Sikh faith echoes this sentiment, praying for blessings to bring prosperity and peace to the world.

Leaders with strong spiritual beliefs often feel that living by their faith brings blessings from God (or a higher power). As one participant put it, "The blessings that I have received are immense... it humbles you." This sense of divine favor inspires them to live a life of kindness and service, not just for personal gain, but also to share these blessings with others. This commitment to the well-being of others aligns with the principles of transformational and interpersonal leadership, where leaders focus on motivating, inspiring, and supporting their employees. The intersection of spiritual blessings and effective leadership offers the potential to foster a better world for individuals, communities, and society at large. The desire to receive divine blessings drives leaders to act with compassion and kindness, making them exemplary leaders in the workplace. Through their actions, they become a source of positivity, satisfaction, and blessings not just for themselves but for everyone they encounter.

◆ ◆ ◆

2. Calmness

A poised and tranquil leader is better suited to confront challenges, make pivotal decisions, and inspire and guide others toward shared objectives. Conversely, leaders who are easily agitated or reactive may foster a hostile work atmosphere, undermine morale, and grapple with achieving their goals. A calm leader is characterized by the ability to maintain composure, even in the face of adversity. This quality empowers them to think clearly and make decisions that best serve their organization and stakeholders. Moreover, this composure can contribute to stress reduction and a more favorable work environment.

Effective leadership is fundamentally about making a constructive impact in the world through astute decision-making and guiding others toward collective objectives. Leaders who cultivate calmness are better equipped to meet these leadership demands by staying calm, focused, and effective under pressure. Cultivating calmness is achievable through a variety of practical strategies. Leaders who integrate mindfulness and meditation into their routines can foster inner peace and equilibrium, enabling them to remain composed during challenges. Regular physical activity can also enhance both physical and emotional well-being, contributing to an overall sense of calmness. Some interviewees shared that their spiritual practices bring them a deep sense of calmness with one interviewee stating that "Being Christian... keeps me happy, confident, and calm. Internally, you're just a calm person." Activities like prayer and meditation often help them feel connected to the divine, fostering serenity and peace.

This emphasis on calmness and composure is a theme found in many religious texts. For example, the Bible encourages turning to prayer to find peace. In Philippians 4:6-7, it says: "Do not be anxious about anything, but in every situation, by prayer and petition, with thanksgiving, present your requests to God. And the peace of God, which transcends all understanding, will guard your hearts and your minds in Christ Jesus." This passage urges reliance on faith to overcome anxiety and find comfort in God's peace. Similarly, Judaism highlights the importance of stillness and reflection to connect with the divine. In Psalm 46:10, it says: "Be still, and know that I am God." This verse underscores the value of pausing and embracing quiet moments to experience inner peace. The Quran also reflects this idea in verse 13:28: "Those who have believed and whose hearts are assured by the remembrance of Allah. Unquestionably, by the remembrance of Allah hearts are assured." Here, the act of remembering God (Allah) is shown as a source of reassurance and tranquility for the heart. These teachings from different traditions illustrate the universal role of spirituality in fostering calmness, helping individuals find peace amidst life's challenges.

The data gleaned from the interviews underscores the connection between spiritual beliefs and calmness, demonstrating that leaders who can maintain composure during high-stress situations are better positioned to exercise control, exercise sound judgment, make informed decisions, and keep their colleagues calm. This attribute significantly contributes to effective leadership and increased organizational productivity. The capacity to maintain calmness through practices like prayer and meditation enables leaders to retain clarity of thought and confidence when making critical decisions in the midst of chaos, ultimately radiating a calming influence that positively impacts their employees who look to them for guidance. The symbiotic relationship between calmness and leadership offers a transformative opportunity for leaders to guide with efficacy. A poised leader can enhance their decision-making capabilities, reduce stress, and cultivate a more favorable work environment. Through their efforts, they can inspire and guide others, fostering a shared sense of purpose and creating a more constructive impact in their organizations and the world.

◆ ◆ ◆

3. Consequences

Behavior modification serves as a valuable tool in steering away from the repercussions of transgressions against one's spiritual beliefs. This process encompasses the identification and transformation of behaviors that lead to sin, ultimately replacing them with healthier and more virtuous actions. Interviewees for this book shared how they changed their behavior to avoid the consequences of sin by following God's teachings, as emphasized in Romans 6:23: "The wages of sin is death, but the free gift of God is eternal life in Christ Jesus our Lord." Similarly, the Quran describes sin as leaving a mark on the heart, which can be cleansed through repentance and forgiveness.

Most major religions are built around the idea of sin and its consequences. Believers often adjust their actions to avoid sin, believing that obedience to their faith leads to salvation. This adjustment not only helps them avoid feelings like guilt or inner conflict but also aligns their lives with their spiritual values and beliefs. The desire to attain salvation through obedience becomes a central motivator.

The research for this book also found that this drive to avoid sin influenced the daily lives and leadership approaches of the interviewees. According to one interviewed leader, "Spirituality makes us cautious of the kind of life we live because we believe that there will be consequences for everything that a man does... man is accountable to either eternal damnation or eternal acceptance into the kingdom of God." Leaders committed to avoiding sin often act with kindness, honesty, and godliness. They follow organizational rules, treat others with empathy, and serve as role models. Their actions align with Interpersonal-Oriented Leadership and Transformational Leadership styles. The research further highlights behavior change as a powerful way to avoid sin's consequences. By practicing self-awareness, taking accountability, and building new habits, individuals strengthen their connection to their faith and live in ways that honor their higher power. This transformation not only supports their spiritual journey but also fosters leadership rooted in empathy, integrity, and strong moral values. Behavior modification may be accomplished through self-awareness, personal accountability, and the cultivation of new habits:

1. Self-Awareness: Acknowledging the importance of self-awareness is essential in modifying behavior. Being aware of one's thoughts, emotions, and actions allows for the identification of factors that may contribute to undesirable conduct. Drawing on biblical references such as Jeremiah 17:9, which highlights the complexity of human nature, supports the premise that recognizing individual weaknesses and vulnerabilities enables the implementation of preventive strategies. Such scriptural insight corresponds with established principles in cognitive behavioral therapy (CBT).

2. Accountability: This concept highlights the

importance of having supportive individuals who can provide accountability, guidance, and encouragement. Drawing from the principles outlined in James 5:16, individuals are encouraged to confide in trusted friends or mentors, thereby creating an environment conducive to healing. Accountability serves as a foundation for support and motivation in overcoming problematic behaviors. This guidance is also consistent with practices found in psychotherapy, counselling, and coaching.

3. Development of New Habits and Practices: Behavior modification includes the cultivation of new habits and practices which aligns with the principles used when trying to grow or increase a person's belief or faith in a religious tradition or higher authority. Such practices may involve activities such as scripture reading and study, participation in religious services, prayer, worship, and engagement in other spiritual disciplines. By following scriptural guidance - for example, the counsel presented in Romans 12:2 - individuals may pursue transformation of thought processes, supporting discernment and alignment with their faith's principles. The recommendations for establishing new habits in this scriptural context also correspond with recognized methods used in psychotherapy practice.

◆ ◆ ◆

4. Decision-Making

The workplace is generally perceived as a non-spiritual environment, where leaders are expected to make pragmatic decisions based on data and facts. However, some leaders have openly acknowledged their practice of prayer before significant business decisions. An interfaith study conducted by Fernando and Jackson in 2006, encompassing Christian, Buddhist, Hindu, and Muslim leaders, revealed a common desire among these leaders to make morally sound decisions aligned with their faith. They sought to lead in a way that upheld the principle of non-maleficence, demonstrating their need for a spiritual connection.

The pursuit of what is deemed "right," as described in the study by Fernando and Jackson, resonates with the experiences of the leaders interviewed in this study and aligns with the Interpersonal-oriented leadership style defined by Eagly and Johnson. Personal spirituality significantly informs the decision-making processes of business leaders for a range of reasons, including the belief in the higher purpose of work, the aspiration to live out one's faith, and the perception of spirituality as a guiding framework for ethical choices.

Business leaders interviewed for this book were guided by their personal spirituality when making decisions, motivated by numerous factors. One interviewee said that "I can take care of the needs of the company but also make decisions that take care of the person as well." Their spirituality provides a moral compass that helps them navigate complex business dilemmas. This influence of spirituality on decision making can be attributed to three core motivations:

1. Work as a Higher Calling: Some business leaders view their work as a higher calling—an opportunity to serve others and create a positive impact in the world. This perspective aligns with the biblical passage from 1 Peter 4:10, emphasizing the use of one's talents to serve others as stewards of God's grace. Decision-making is therefore rooted in the desire to serve and contribute positively.

2. Work as an Act of Faith: For others, their work is

a means of living out their faith and honoring God in every aspect of their lives. This is encapsulated by the biblical principle from 1 Corinthians 10:31, which encourages doing all things to the glory of God. Consequently, business leaders approach their work as a platform to honor and reflect God's values.

3. Spirituality as a Framework for Ethical Decisions: Personal spirituality is seen as a source of wisdom and ethical guidance. Leaders turn to their spirituality for insight and understanding, believing it can help them make sound ethical decisions. Proverbs 2:6 in the Bible attests to this, stating that wisdom and understanding come from the Lord.

In essence, decision-making is a pivotal aspect of effective leadership, and several leaders interviewed for this book emphasized the role of spirituality in guiding their decision-making processes. Some leaders mentioned turning to prayer, particularly when confronted with challenging business decisions. Other religious books like the Quran also talk about making decisions. For leaders who are religious, the Quran, Bible, Torah and other religious books serve as key guides, showing how important it is to seek God's help when deciding what to do when making personal and business decisions.

◆ ◆ ◆

5. Dissonance

Dissonance occurs when a business leader's spiritual beliefs and values conflict with their business goals, causing discomfort, anxiety, and tension that impacts the decision-making process.

There are two primary ways in which spiritual dissonance can influence business decisions:

1. Conflict Between Beliefs and Objectives: Spiritual dissonance may arise when business objectives clash with a leader's deeply held spiritual values. For instance, a business leader may face a decision that could boost profits but contradicts their spiritual principles. This conflict may lead to dissonance as they grapple with the desire to succeed in business while remaining faithful to their spiritual beliefs. Consequently, they may prioritize decisions that align with their personal values, even at the expense of certain business objectives.

2. Reflective and Mindful Decision-Making: Conversely, spiritual dissonance can encourage a more introspective and considered approach to decision-making. Confronted with conflicting values, a business leader may embark on a journey of self-reflection to gain a deeper understanding of their spiritual beliefs and values. This reflection often results in a more profound understanding of their personal spirituality and, consequently, influences their decision-making. They may be more inclined to make choices that harmonize with their spiritual beliefs, even if this entails sacrificing certain business goals.

In essence, to minimize dissonance these leaders base their decisions on the answer to the question" what would God do?" Research has demonstrated that spiritual beliefs play a pivotal role in decision-making across various contexts. For example, a study published in the Journal of Business Ethics identified the influence of spiritual beliefs on ethical decision-making among business leaders in India. The research showed that leaders who placed a higher value on spirituality were more likely to make ethical decisions, even when it meant compromising some business objectives (Jain, 2011).

Leaders who aim to avoid spiritual dissonance by adhering to their spirituality often engage in behavior modification to reconcile their actions with their beliefs. This frequently involves treating employees with empathy, dignity, and respect, leading with honesty, and adhering to ethical conduct. This was exemplified by an interviewee whose ability to forgive and seek forgiveness helped alleviate guilt and brought her peace, enabling her to "look at myself in the mirror and say I'm not guilty of anything." This the research reveals that personal spirituality influences ethical decisions, as leaders strive to avoid dissonance by aligning their actions with their deeply held spiritual values, ultimately contributing to the development of good leadership characterized by traits such as empathy, peace, and honesty.

◆ ◆ ◆

6. Equality

The leaders interviewed for this book said their spiritual beliefs strongly motivate them to promote equality in how they lead and treat others. Here, equality means treating everyone the same, without any unfairness or discrimination. This idea comes from many religions and is similar to the golden rule: treat others as you want to be treated. Sikhism, founded by Guru Nanak, places a strong emphasis on the equality of all people. Sikhism practices include supporting the needy and providing daily meals without regard to a person's race, religion, or gender. A Sikh leader interviewed for this book described her commitment to being a "saint-soldier," combining compassion and protection for her staff and others. She emphasized the idea that every Sikh is meant to be a "saint" who does good deeds and promotes peace and, if necessary, becomes a "soldier" to defend equality and justice, not just for themselves but for any defenseless person. The democratic leadership style of Guru Gobind Singh is also highlighted, which emphasizes equality between men and women within Sikhism. Equality is also a biblical principle, as evidenced in Deuteronomy (10:17), emphasizing that God shows no partiality and accepts no bribes. Similarly, the Quran references equality, stating that "male or female, you are equal to one another" (Quran 3:195).

Leaders in this book, whose spirituality motivated them to seek equality treated their team members fairly and respectfully. This likely led to fewer complaints to HR and more engaged workers, as employees felt valued and respected. This kind of leadership creates a better, more positive work environment, where employees feel motivated and supported. This, in turn, boosts productivity and job satisfaction, as employees are more likely to be engaged and committed to their work. These leaders draw upon their spiritual beliefs to create a more just and inclusive work environment, ultimately benefiting both employees and the organization. The pursuit of equality is a unifying principle across different faiths and a powerful source of inspiration for leaders seeking to make a positive impact in their workplaces. According to one interviewed leader: "Humility keeps me grounded, helping me to see others as equals and to avoid any impression of being superior or authoritarian."

◆ ◆ ◆

7. Fairness

The multifaceted nature of leadership underscores the importance of fairness as a fundamental character trait that influences effective leadership. Fairness, defined as treating individuals with respect and equality, devoid of bias or discrimination, is explored in the context of both spiritual and non-spiritual leaders. Studies show that fairness is not only an essential component of ethical leadership but also an element that fosters trust, respect, and cooperation among team members.

Leaders who integrate their spiritual beliefs into their leadership often hold fairness in high regard. They seek to create workplaces that reflect a sense of meaning and purpose in their work and the work of others. For spiritual leaders, fairness is a way to ensure that they embody the principles of their faith, thereby contributing to a more just and equitable work environment that supports the well-being and development of all employees.

Spiritual leaders who uphold fairness exert a profound influence on the culture of their organizations. They create an environment where everyone feels valued, respected, and supported, thus leading to higher levels of motivation, engagement, and productivity. Such leaders foster an atmosphere of trust and openness, where employees feel comfortable sharing their ideas, concerns, and feedback. They also promote a sense of community where everyone is dedicated to common goals and works together as a cohesive unit.

Fair leaders also champion transparency and accountability within their organizations, thereby building trust and credibility. They set clear and consistent policies and procedures, ensure that everyone comprehends them, and hold themselves and others accountable for adhering to them. Constructive feedback is a cornerstone of their leadership style, where superior performance is recognized and rewarded, and areas of improvement are addressed in a supportive and respectful manner. Some of the interviewed leaders shared their experiences of modifying their behavior to align with their spiritual beliefs, particularly in cases of bias or favoritism. This adjustment helps these leaders counter their natural inclination to favor those who share similar characteristics, beliefs, or backgrounds.

Religious texts like the Bible and the Quran stress the importance of being fair. For example, Romans 2:11 says, "For God shows no partiality," emphasizing fairness. In Islam, justice and fairness are key parts of religious practice. This backs up the research finding that fairness is essential for successful leaders, whether they are religious or not. Fairness builds trust, respect, and teamwork, leading to better organizational performance and positive results. Research also suggest that leaders who are fair not only act ethically but also create environments where their team members can thrive. For spiritually driven leaders, fairness is a core value that fits with their goal of leading justly and equitably as exemplified by one interviewee who stated that: "When you and I have a contract, there must be fairness, integrity, and dutifulness regardless of what's happening."

Fairness is a cornerstone of many religions and philosophies. It is often seen as a reflection of divine attributes and a path to moral and spiritual growth. Fair leaders inspire trust and loyalty among their followers, creating a strong sense of community and purpose. They also promote a culture of respect and understanding, which can help to resolve conflicts peacefully and build bridges between diverse groups. In addition to its spiritual and ethical significance, fairness is also essential for practical reasons. Fair leaders are more likely to make sound decisions, as they are able to consider all sides of an issue and avoid bias. They are also more likely to be effective communicators, as they are able to articulate their ideas clearly and persuasively.

As a result, fair leaders are often able to achieve their goals more efficiently and effectively than those who are not. Fairness is a vital quality for leaders of all kinds. It reflects our highest values and a powerful tool for building strong, positive relationships. By striving to be fair in our words and deeds, we can create a better world for all.

◆ ◆ ◆

8. Faith

The intricate world of leadership emphasizes the significance of how faith as a character trait profoundly influences leaders, particularly those who are spiritual. Faith, a deeply personal and powerful force, offers individuals a sense of purpose, meaning, and direction, ultimately impacting a leader's ability to inspire, motivate, and guide others. Faith can be defined as a belief or trust in something beyond oneself, often associated with a higher power or divine source. For spiritual leaders, faith is a cornerstone of their identity, shaping their values, beliefs, and worldview. This foundational belief motivates them to serve others and uphold values such as integrity, compassion, and service.

Spiritual leaders who embody faith as a character trait often serve as role models and mentors, inspiring others to reach their full potential and pursue their aspirations. They lead by example, demonstrating commitment to their values and faith-inspired principles. Their actions are marked by humility, empathy, and respect, fostering a positive and supportive environment where team members feel valued and motivated.

Faith-driven leaders often possess the ability to see beyond immediate obstacles and challenges. They maintain a long-term perspective that centers on the greater good, inspiring hope and optimism within their teams even during adversity. Drawing strength and resilience from their faith, they preserve their sense of purpose and direction, grounded in their core values.

Faith-based leaders tend to display a deep sense of humility and gratitude. They acknowledge that their success is not solely of their making and readily appreciate the contributions of others. This fosters a culture of collaboration and teamwork, underpinned by mutual support and respect. These leaders also prioritize personal and professional balance, recognizing the importance of self-care and the cultivation of meaningful relationships.

For many leaders in this study, their faith is integral to their identity, shaping their behavior in both personal and professional spheres. Identifying with their faith is a strong motivational factor, inspiring them to align their actions with their spirituality and demonstrate reverence to their creator or God. In the Quran, Surat An-Nisa (4:136) emphasizes faith in Allah, while the Bible in Hebrews 11:1 describes faith as the assurance of things hoped for and the conviction of things not seen. This is demonstrated by one leader whose trust grew through her experiences of God's faithfulness, as she stated, "I can look back and see how faithful He's been... and why is He going to stop now?" Research, such as Marinoble's 1991 study, suggests that the development of faith, often stemming from a person's spirituality, forms the foundation of the transformational leadership style. This style aligns with the interpersonal oriented and inclusive leadership model demonstrated by the leaders interviewed for this book.

Faith inspires individuals on a quest for purposes that extends beyond themselves, leading to a sense of responsibility for others in their community. Ultimately, faith enhances leadership by promoting positive behavior towards others, translating to a more harmonious work environment, reduced stress among employees, greater teamwork, and improved business performance. Faith is a pivotal character trait for spiritual leaders who aspire to inspire, motivate, and guide others. Leaders with faith have a unique ability to maintain a long-term perspective, inspire hope, and create a collaborative and supportive work environment. Their leadership is marked by humility, empathy, and respect, aligning with the values of the interpersonal oriented leadership model. Faith is an influential force that profoundly affects how spiritual leaders guide and manage their organizations, offering a sense of purpose, meaning, and direction that can inspire others to excel.

◆ ◆ ◆

9. Forgiveness

Forgiveness, a deeply personal and transformative force, offers individuals a profound sense of peace, healing, and personal growth. It has a substantial impact on a leader's ability to inspire and motivate their teams. Forgiveness is defined as the act of releasing resentment, anger, or negative emotions towards someone who has wronged us. It is deeply intertwined with spirituality and is seen as a path to achieving inner peace and healing in the face of hurt and betrayal. For spiritual leaders, forgiveness is integral to their identity, shaping their values, beliefs, and worldviews. These leaders are driven by the pursuit of peace and personal growth, acting as powerful motivators for those under their guidance.

Leaders who embody forgiveness as a character trait are often seen as inspirational figures and mentors, motivating others to embrace forgiveness, both in giving and seeking. They lead by example, manifesting a commitment to values such as compassion, empathy, and respect. Their actions underscore the importance of humility, kindness, and empathy, fostering a positive and supportive atmosphere where team members feel cherished and motivated.

Leaders with forgiveness as a character trait also foster an environment characterized by trust, respect, and collaboration. This environment nurtures healthy relationships among team members. These leaders are willing to admit mistakes and failures, and they readily extend and seek forgiveness, thus establishing a culture of accountability and growth. This, in turn, enables them to maintain a sense of purpose and direction that remains grounded in their core values, even in challenging times.

Leaders with forgiveness as a character trait typically have a deep sense of gratitude, acknowledging that forgiveness is a transformative gift capable of mending relationships, strengthening teams, and fortifying organizations. They readily express their gratitude towards those who have forgiven them and can generously extend forgiveness to others, even when it is a difficult endeavor. These leaders emphasize the importance of balance in their personal and professional lives, appreciating the need for self-care and the cultivation of meaningful relationships.

Several of the interviewed leaders emphasized the importance of forgiveness, particularly in the context of seeking forgiveness from God. Forgiveness is considered an essential gateway to salvation among those of the Christian and Islamic faiths. The belief in forgiveness as a means to salvation profoundly influences the behavior of these leaders, who strive to live kindly and virtuously, embodying their roles as leaders within their teams and organizations. One interviewed leader expressed daily gratitude to God and sought forgiveness both from God and other people. He said, "I believe in forgiving and forgetting. I may not forget, but I'm willing to forgive and move on."

Scriptural references from various religions underscore the significance of forgiveness. In the Bible, Matthew 26:28 conveys the message of forgiveness as the means to pardon sins. The Quran, in Chapter 39:53, emphasizes Allah's limitless forgiveness, echoing the theme of redemption through forgiveness. Sikhism, as portrayed in Guru Granth Sahib (1372), underlines the transformative power of forgiveness. Additionally, studies like the one conducted by Cameron and Caza emphasize the virtues of organizational leadership, and the role played by forgiveness. They introduce the concept of "organizational forgiveness" as a vital element in effective leadership, thereby validating the experiences and outcomes shared by the leaders interviewed in this study.

This research supports the idea that forgiveness, influenced by spirituality, plays an integral role in leadership effectiveness. Interview data from this research suggests that forgiveness is a critical character trait for spiritual leaders who aspire to inspire, motivate, and guide others. Leaders who possess forgiveness as a character trait can create an environment that fosters trust, respect, and collaboration, nurturing healthy relationships within their teams. Their readiness to admit mistakes and extend forgiveness establishes a culture of accountability and growth. They also cultivate gratitude and maintain balance in their personal and professional lives. Ultimately, forgiveness is a powerful force that guides spiritual leaders in creating peace, healing, and personal growth within their organizations.

◆ ◆ ◆

10. Gratefulness

Gratefulness is a quality that resonates deeply with spirituality. Many of the interviewed leaders revealed how gratefulness is intricately linked to their spirituality. These leaders express their gratitude through prayer, acknowledging the blessings they have received from a divine source. Gratefulness becomes a bridge connecting the material world with spiritual beliefs, cultivating a profound sense of appreciation.

Gratefulness is a fundamental concept in several religions. The Bible, Deuteronomy 8:7-10, instructs believers to give thanks for the bounties of the earth. The Quran emphasizes that gratitude leads to abundance. Jewish teachings center around giving thanks to God, woven into the very fabric of their way of life. Sikhism encourages an attitude of gratitude, with Guru Nanak highlighting the importance of recognizing and appreciating the gifts one has received. These scriptures underline the intrinsic connection between spirituality and gratefulness, shaping the behavior and values of believers. This was described by one leader saying, "it's not complicated, you spend your days serving others, and ... being in that state of gratitude."

Gratefulness is not confined to religious contexts; it is also a fundamental concept in positive psychology. Gratitude, in this sense, is the act of expressing appreciation for the valuable things in life. Emmons, in 2004, described gratitude as a positive emotion experienced upon giving or receiving something of value. It is a potent force that promotes a sense of well-being and fosters positive connections.

Gratefulness is not just a personal virtue; it has profound implications for leadership. Research, such as the study conducted by Garg and Gera, has explored the mediating role of social intelligence in the relationship between gratitude and leadership. Leaders who express appreciation to their employees, even when remunerated for their work, foster a culture of gratitude. In turn, this appreciation motivates employees to excel, leading to increased productivity, enhanced morale, and improved overall profitability in the organizations where these leaders serve.

Research by Garg and Gera (2019) highlights the transformative power of gratefulness as a character trait. It serves as a conduit between the material world and spirituality, enriching the lives of those who embrace it. Gratefulness permeates religious texts, promoting behaviors aligned with spirituality. In both religious and secular contexts, it emerges as a fundamental concept that enhances well-being, fosters positive relationships, and even elevates leadership. Leaders who incorporate gratefulness into their leadership style cultivate a culture of appreciation, motivating their teams to excel and thereby elevating organizational success. Gratefulness is not merely an expression of thanks; it is a powerful force that shapes lives, enriches experiences, and inspires greatness as exemplified by participant 5 who begins and ends his days in prayer, offering thanks to God.

❖ ❖ ❖

11. Honesty

Honesty, a potent and transformative quality, profoundly influences how leaders guide and motivate their teams, manage organizations, and cultivate a culture steeped in trust and respect. Honesty is defined as the quality of being truthful, transparent, and sincere. It involves conducting oneself with integrity, ethics, and values aligned with one's beliefs and morals. For spiritual leaders, honesty is integral to their identity, shaping their values, beliefs, and worldviews. Leaders with honesty as a character trait are often driven by an unwavering sense of integrity and accountability, motivating those they lead. Leaders embodying honesty as a character trait are often considered inspirational figures and mentors, motivating others to emulate their example. They lead by exemplifying values such as transparency, accountability, and respect. Their honesty inspires them to act with humility, compassion, and empathy toward others, fostering a positive and nurturing environment where team members feel valued and encouraged.

Leaders with honesty as a character trait can cultivate an environment of trust, respect, and collaboration, nourishing healthy relationships among team members. They are unafraid to acknowledge mistakes and failures, assuming responsibility and accountability. This culture of transparency and growth empowers them to maintain a sense of purpose and direction that remains rooted in their core values, even during challenging periods.

Leaders who embrace honesty as a character trait often possess a deep sense of self-awareness, acknowledging their strengths and weaknesses. They are committed to continuous self-improvement and strive to develop their organization. Honesty empowers them to communicate candidly and authentically, cultivating an environment of open communication and trust. These leaders are also conscious of the significance of equilibrium in their personal and professional lives. They value their well-being and recognize its impact on their ability to lead and maintain a sense of balance in their leadership. Many leaders interviewed for this study spoke about the centrality of honesty in their faith and daily lives. One leader that was interviewed, maintained honesty at all times in her business, saying "We keep clean books… we don't have cash under the table."

Honesty is regarded as a virtuous character trait, characterized by truthfulness in all circumstances. It occupies a pivotal place in spirituality and is central to numerous religious doctrines. The Bible offers several references to honesty. Proverbs 14:5 state, "An honest witness does not deceive, but a false witness pours out lies." Furthermore, Jesus referred to himself as "the Way, the Truth, and the Life," affirming the significance of honesty for Christians. Deception, seen as un-Christlike, is considered sinful and could have eternal consequences, such as hell, if God does not grant forgiveness according to the Bible and the Christian faith. The Quran, like the Bible, emphasizes honesty. In al-Tawbah 9:119, believers are encouraged to be among "the truthful ones."

Research also validated data from the interviewees and scriptures. Notably, research has explored the relationship between honesty and leadership. Kirkpatrick and Locke's 1991 study, which delved into the influence of personal traits on leadership, identified honesty and integrity among the personality traits that aid leaders in acquiring necessary skills, developing plans, acquiring organizational vision, and formulating the strategies required to turn these visions into reality. This documented correlation between honesty and effective leadership substantiates the experiences and outcomes shared by the leaders interviewed for this book and reinforces the notion that honesty, fueled by spirituality, is a significant personality trait of highly effective leaders.

Honesty is an indispensable character trait for spiritual leaders who aspire to guide, inspire, and lead their teams effectively. Leaders with honesty as a character trait are capable of cultivating an environment imbued with trust, respect, and collaboration, fostering healthy relationships among team members. Their willingness to accept accountability and admit mistakes creates a culture of transparency and growth. They encourage self-awareness, open communication, and value the importance of maintaining a sense of equilibrium in their leadership. Ultimately, honesty stands as a compelling force that profoundly influences how spiritual leaders manage their organizations, inspire their teams, and create a culture founded on trust and respect.

◆ ◆ ◆

12. Leadership Styles

This book, through the analysis of interview data, explores the dynamic relationship between spirituality and leadership styles, emphasizing the crucial role of integrating these aspects to create effective, values-driven leadership. Spirituality plays a significant role in how leaders' function within their organizations. It provides leaders with a guiding framework shaped by purpose, values, and beliefs. Research by Robert Emmons suggests that spirituality enhances leadership by fostering positive emotions, trust-building, and community creation. Incorporating spirituality into leadership is linked to enhanced employee well-being, job satisfaction, ethical behavior, and overall organizational effectiveness. By balancing task accomplishment with relationship-building and recognizing the unique needs of individual team members, leaders can create a more personalized and effective approach to leadership. Integrating spirituality into leadership provides a sense of purpose, guiding principles, and community development within the organization.

Interpersonal-oriented leadership styles, such as

transformational, democratic, and servant leadership, embody spiritual values like empathy, compassion, and service. One leader noted, "When you are people-focused...you have to change your style... The Holy Spirit is...the conscience before you do anything that is evil; he will prompt you, 'Oh, that's not right." Servant leaders prioritize relationship-building, empower team members, and promote growth and development. Simultaneously, they are goal-oriented, emphasize accountability, and achieve results. Most leaders interviewed for this book aligned with the Interpersonal-oriented leadership style, demonstrating that it is closely aligned with spiritual beliefs. This alignment is evident in leaders who genuinely care about their team members, utilizing empathy, fairness, and loyalty in their approach to accomplish tasks. In contrast, Task-oriented leaders tend to focus solely on task completion, often lacking empathy and care for team members. However, this results-oriented leadership approach can be essential in professions or situations where the consequences of failure, or the need for timely and accurate task execution, take precedence over fostering employee relationships.

The individuals profiled in this book can benefit from integrating Interpersonal-oriented and Task-oriented leadership styles to enhance leadership effectiveness, employee well-being, ethical behavior, and overall organizational performance. By balancing results and relationships, while acknowledging the unique needs and motivations of team members, these leaders can create a personalized and effective leadership approach.

◆ ◆ ◆

13. Learning

The capacity for continual learning is an essential characteristic for successful leadership. Leaders who embrace a commitment to learning are not only open to innovative ideas and adaptable to change but also have the capacity to inspire those they lead to grow and develop. In the context of spiritual leadership, learning takes on even greater significance as it aligns with the principles of personal growth and self-discovery. The data from this research and other studies emphasizes the impact of learning on self-awareness, sense of purpose, and organizational growth.

Spiritual leaders who value learning prioritize self-reflection and self-awareness. They recognize that their personal beliefs and values deeply influence their leadership style. By engaging in continuous self-reflection, they gain a profound understanding of their strengths and weaknesses, enabling them to lead authentically with compassion and empathy. This authentic leadership fosters trust and loyalty among their followers.

Spiritual leaders understand that their role transcends mere management or profitability. They realize that their work carries a broader impact on the world. By learning about their employees, customers, and stakeholders, spiritual leaders gain insights into their needs and aspirations. This knowledge allows them to develop strategies that align with their values and goals, creating a profound sense of purpose and meaning in their leadership. This newfound sense of purpose not only motivates leaders but also inspires their followers to work toward a common, meaningful goal.

Learning empowers spiritual leaders to establish a culture of continuous improvement within their organizations. They recognize that their employees are their most valuable assets and are committed to helping them learn and grow. By offering opportunities for training and development, spiritual leaders cultivate a learning environment where employees can enhance their skills and knowledge. This culture of continuous improvement benefits employees personally and helps organizations remain competitive and adaptable in ever-changing market conditions.

The leaders interviewed for this book shared a common trait of continuous learning, which greatly contributed to their growth. They consistently sought to expand their knowledge and enhance their practices. Various religious texts encourage this pursuit of learning. For instance, Proverbs (1:5) states, "Let the wise hear and increase in learning, and the one who understands obtain guidance." The Quran (20:114) similarly notes, "...'My Lord, increase me in knowledge'." These references underscore the value of ongoing education. One interviewee said: "There is so much depth in my [religious] practice that I'm always learning. It's a lifetime job."

Additionally, contemporary leadership research has also identified a strong connection between learning and effective leadership. Studies such as the one conducted by Lillas Brown and Barry Posner emphasize the role of active learning in leadership engagement and effectiveness. This research highlights that individuals who identify as active learners tend to be more involved and engaged leaders. Hence, the commitment to learning in one's faith may also extend to professional development, enhancing their knowledge and performance in their respective fields.

Learning is not just a trait but a foundation for effective leadership, particularly within the realm of spiritual leadership. By prioritizing self-reflection, fostering a sense of purpose, and instilling a culture of continuous improvement, spiritual leaders are better equipped to lead with authenticity, compassion, and empathy.

◆ ◆ ◆

14. Loyalty

Loyalty is a reciprocal commitment, a bridge of trust that connects leaders and their employees. In the realm of spiritual leadership, this understanding holds even more weight. Spiritual leaders prioritize relationships, recognize their responsibility in initiating loyalty, and work to align the entire organization with a shared sense of purpose through a two-way commitment that involves initiating loyalty, commitment to the greater good, and transparency and honesty. Even when leaders feel their loyalty is not reciprocated by their organization, some remain committed. One leader stated, "There is no sense of loyalty from a corporation, but I love what I do".

Spiritual leaders understand that loyalty starts with them. They are dedicated to living out their core values and beliefs, leading by example. The needs of their employees are paramount, and they strive to create an environment where employees feel valued and supported. By doing so, a sense of loyalty is nurtured, where employees commit not only to their leader but also to the organization.

Loyalty extends to a commitment to the organization's greater good. Spiritual leaders perceive their role as one of service to the organization's mission and purpose. They align their own goals with this mission and effectively communicate it to their employees. This shared sense of purpose breeds a culture of loyalty, where employees dedicate themselves to the organization's success, transcending individual interests.

Loyalty is inherently linked to transparency and honesty. Spiritual leaders comprehend that trust is founded on transparency and they proactively create an environment in which employees feel comfortable sharing concerns and ideas. They openly discuss the challenges facing the organization and collaborate with their employees to identify solutions.

This transparency fosters a profound sense of loyalty, where employees feel valued and respected, strengthening their commitment to the organization's success. Loyalty, within the context of spirituality, was highlighted by several participants in this study. These individuals exemplified loyalty to God and to one another as an expression of their faith. They believe in demonstrating loyalty to God through their actions, minimizing the dissonance of acting disloyally to their faith. Scriptures such as 2 Samuel (16:17) and Proverbs (21:21) encourage loyalty to God and others, serving as guiding principles for their conduct.

Incorporating contemporary research, a study by Huaiyong Wang, Guangli Lu, and Yongfang Liu found a positive relationship between ethical leadership and loyalty, particularly in the context of China. This research reinforces the significant role of ethical leadership. This is because loyalty is not only a desirable trait but a critical one for effective leadership, particularly for those who are spiritual leaders. By placing relationships at the forefront, embodying their values, and committing to the greater good of the organization, spiritual leaders cultivate a culture of loyalty, forging trust and dedication. This loyalty extends beyond the leader's own benefit; it motivates employees to work collaboratively towards a common goal, thereby generating a positive impact on their organization.

◆ ◆ ◆

15. Meditation

Meditation, a practice with history spanning centuries, has long been employed as a means for individuals to forge a connection with their inner selves, alleviate stress, and enhance their overall well-being. Recently, it has garnered substantial attention within the business world, with many leaders adopting meditation to refine their leadership skills and bolster their organization.

Meditation involves the art of quieting the mind and immersing oneself in the present moment. Extensive research attests to its efficacy in diminishing stress and anxiety, heightening focus and concentration, and elevating self-awareness. Spiritual leaders acknowledge the profound significance of this practice, not only for their personal growth but also for their capacity to lead with distinction.

Meditation empowers spiritual leaders to establish a tranquil and clear state of mind. Through this practice, they nurture self-awareness, recognize their own biases and limitations, and gain a deeper understanding of their employees' needs. This heightened self-awareness equips them to lead with authenticity, empathy, and compassion. The practice of meditation also equips spiritual leaders to regulate their emotions and make more informed decisions. It enables them to become fully present in the moment, thus responding to situations with enhanced clarity and focus. By making decisions from a place of serenity and lucidity, spiritual leaders can lead their organizations with confidence.

Spiritual leaders, through their meditation practice, can instill a culture of mindfulness within their organizations. Leading by example, they encourage employees to allocate time for themselves and prioritize their well-being. This culture of mindfulness not only benefits employees but also augments the organization's resilience and adaptability in the face of change.

While few study participants shared their use of meditation as a coping mechanism in both their personal and professional lives, meditation is an integral practice for achieving spiritual awareness and connection with the transcendent. Mindfulness techniques enhance focus, attention, and awareness, leading to greater mental clarity, emotional equilibrium, and spiritual fulfillment. This is exemplified by participant 2 who coped with stress through prayer and meditation. "When I'm working out in the gym, it becomes a place of meditation... you'll never feel the stress, or worries, or anxiety ever again."

References to meditation can be found in several religious texts. In the Bible, Psalm (19:14) proclaims, "Let the words of my mouth and the meditation of my heart be acceptable in your sight, O Lord, my rock and my redeemer." In Joshua (1:8), it is stated, "This Book of the Law shall not depart from your mouth, but you shall meditate on it day and night, so that you may be careful to do according to all that is written in it." Similarly, the Quran (17:79) advises, "During the night, you shall meditate for extra credit, that your Lord may raise you to an honorable rank." Sikhism also references meditation in Guru Granth Sahib (Japji, p. 1) as it emphasizes the need for the Love of the Almighty as an integral component of meditation. Traditions such as Buddhism are also renowned for their utilization of meditation as a conduit to heightened enlightenment.

Furthermore, contemporary research, such as McCullum's 1999 study, underscores the connection between meditation and leadership behavior. Subjects who practiced meditation using the Transcendental Meditation method, as part of their spirituality, displayed improved leadership behaviors. This underscores how leaders who incorporate meditation into their spiritual practices not only cope more effectively in their personal lives but also enhance their leadership capabilities, translating to superior job performance.

Meditation emerges as a potent tool that profoundly shapes the leadership and management approach of spiritual leaders. By facilitating an intimate connection with their inner selves, enabling emotion management, and fostering a culture of mindfulness, spiritual leaders lead with authenticity, empathy, and compassion. This practice not only empowers the leader but also engenders a nurturing and supportive environment for employees, culminating in a more engaged and productive workforce.

◆ ◆ ◆

16. Obedience

Leadership is a multifaceted skill that demands a harmonious blend of diverse traits and qualities to be truly successful. Among these essential traits, obedience may appear counterintuitive to some, often conjuring notions of submissiveness or weakness. However, spiritual leaders recognize its paramount significance in the art of leading and managing organizations.

Obedience is a quality often associated with mere compliance and submission. However, spiritual leaders comprehend that obedience is not synonymous with blindly following rules or commands. Instead, it embodies profound respect for authority and a wholehearted willingness to submit to the greater good of the organization. These leaders recognize that their purpose revolves around serving the mission and purpose of the organization. Consequently, they actively work to align their personal goals with this overarching mission. This sense of obedience serves as a guiding light, helping leaders maintain unwavering focus on the organization's objectives, and inspires them to lead by example.

For many study participants, obedience was a fundamental aspect of their lives, intricately linked to their commitment to following the tenets of their faith. Some prioritized their obedience to God above their professional responsibilities, while others placed the Ten Commandments at the forefront of their ethical framework, surpassing business policies, procedures, or regulations. In the business context, participant 4 exemplified this obedience, motivated by fear of consequences for disobedience: "There are consequences to people's actions... in the long run, we are judged by our acts of obedience to God." This steadfast obedience resonates with the essence of spirituality, entailing a belief in and connection with the transcendent or God. Consequently, spiritual individuals are inherently believers, devoted to following the doctrines of their faith.

Deviation from obedience, particularly concerning religious or spiritual beliefs, can evoke cognitive dissonance among leaders. This dissonance arises from internal conflict, guilt, or remorse stemming from business decisions that are incongruent with their spiritual beliefs. Chronic cognitive dissonance often culminates in anxiety and depression, precipitated by the mental and emotional stress and discomfort associated with the perception of wrongdoing or a misalignment with their values, morals, or spiritual beliefs.

References to obedience can be found in various religious scriptures, illustrating its intrinsic role in spiritual practice. The Bible, for instance, highlights the contrast between disobedience and righteousness, emphasizing that obedience leads to righteousness (Romans 5:19). It also cites Jesus as a model of obedience (Philippians 2:8). Similarly, the Quran emphasizes obedience to what is right (Quran [24:54]). Obedience is a key aspect in other religions, including Judaism, Sikhism, Hinduism, and the Orisha religion of the Yoruba people, highlighting its universal importance in spirituality.

Empirical research also demonstrates the impact of obedience on leadership. Blind obedience, often associated with tyrannical leaders, can yield negative consequences, as exemplified by the atrocities committed during the Second World War under Adolf Hitler's leadership. These instances underscore how obedience to unscrupulous leaders can result in significant harm and unjust actions. However, obedience, when rooted in true spirituality tends to encourage ethical behavior, aligning decisions with scripture or religious tenets. Leaders who are spiritual aspire to harmonize their organizational policies with their spiritual beliefs whenever possible, creating a cohesive environment that aligns personal values and business practices. Notably, U.S. fast-food chain Chick-fil-A chooses to close on Sundays in observance of the Sabbath, exemplifying the attempt to harmonize business decisions with spiritual convictions.

Obedience stands as a vital trait for effective leadership, particularly among leaders who are spiritual. By fostering profound respect for authority, wholehearted commitment to the organization's greater good, and modeling ethical leadership, spiritual leaders cultivate a culture rooted in trust and respect within their organizations. This culture does not merely benefit the leaders themselves but also serves as a wellspring of inspiration for their employees, uniting them in the pursuit of a shared vision and fostering a positive impact on the world.

◆ ◆ ◆

17. Optimism

Leadership, a multifaceted and intricate skill, calls for an amalgamation of diverse traits and qualities. Among these, optimism, characterized by a hopeful and positive outlook, stands out as a fundamental trait. Optimistic leaders who are spiritual possess an unwavering faith in the future, irrespective of the adversities they face. This radiant attitude is, in itself, contagious, inspiring their employees to embrace a similar mindset. By maintaining this positive outlook, these leaders serve as a beacon of inspiration for their teams, encouraging them to remain steadfast and motivated, even in the face of daunting challenges. Furthermore, the optimism exuded by these leaders fosters a culture of innovation and creativity within the organization, as employees feel empowered to take risks and explore new ideas. Optimism empowers leaders who are spiritual to perceive challenges as opportunities for growth and advancement. Instead of being disheartened by setbacks or obstacles, they embrace these as invaluable experiences for learning and development. These leaders actively seek lessons within each challenge and utilize this newfound wisdom to make informed decisions and enhance the organization's operations.

Optimistic leaders have the remarkable ability to infuse their organizations with a profound sense of hope and purpose. Their unwavering positive outlook keeps employees focused on the mission and purpose of the organization. This sense of purpose serves as a driving force, motivating employees to collectively work towards shared objectives. The result is an engaged and committed workforce, dedicated to the organization's greater vision. Participant 2 is an optimistic leader who emphasized that "A Sikh is always in a state of optimism," describing "Chardi Kala" as her guiding principle and she works to cultivate this optimism in her team as a way of building trust and accountability.

In the ever-changing landscape of leadership, optimism equips leaders with the resilience and perseverance required to navigate the inevitable highs and lows. They stand resolutely in the face of adversity, maintaining an air of calm and stability within their organizations. Their optimism serves as a guiding light through the storm, enabling them to emerge stronger on the other side. Optimism finds its roots in the realm of spirituality and faith, encapsulating a belief in a brighter future or positive outcomes, underpinned by trust in the transcendent, a higher power, or nature—whatever an individual's chosen object of reverence may be. Numerous faiths prescribe optimism as a way of life for their followers. For example, Sikhs are encouraged to perpetually inhabit a state of "Chardi kala," signifying a perpetual upward ascent of the spirit. Similarly, Christianity fosters optimism through verses such as Philippians 4:13, emphasizing empowerment through faith. Islam propagates optimism by urging perseverance during challenging times, as indicated by the Quran (94:5-6). This shared emphasis on optimism across various faiths explains why leaders who are spiritual often radiate positivity. The promises and teachings within religious texts form the bedrock of the profound self-confidence and positive outlook that many spiritual leaders project. This optimism significantly informs their leadership style.

Empirical research affirms the strong correlation between optimism and transformational leadership, the prevailing style among leaders in this study who identify as spiritual. Leaders in this category inspire trust and confidence among their employees by projecting a positive vision for the future and collaborating with their teams to pave the way towards shared objectives. Optimistic leaders are not only well-liked by their teams but also possess the ability to breed trust within their organizations, which often translates to operational and business success. Their infectious energy and unwavering commitment to their vision captivate their employees, leading to a more productive work environment. When a leader radiates positivity, employees become wholehearted supporters of the shared vision, contributing their best efforts to realize it. This quality is particularly invaluable in startups and emerging organizations where a leader's optimism becomes the driving force for achieving the company's goals.

Optimism is a powerful force in spiritual leadership, shaping how dedicated leaders guide their organizations. By viewing challenges as growth opportunities, fostering hope and purpose, and modeling resilience, they inspire teams, spark innovation, and drive success. Ultimately, their unwavering optimism lights the way forward.

◆ ◆ ◆

18. Peace

Leadership is a multifaceted journey, requiring a diverse blend of qualities. Among these, the trait of tranquility, found in peaceful leaders who are spiritual, stands as a fundamental attribute. Peaceful leaders who are spiritual radiate a calm and centered presence, a rare quality that remains unwavering in the face of conflict and chaos. Their ability to create an environment of peace and serenity within their organizations cannot be understated. This serenity has the power to profoundly impact the culture and morale of their workforce. Moreover, their composed presence empowers them to make informed decisions and maintain a clear sense of purpose even in the midst of challenging situations.

These leaders also have a unique gift for fostering harmony and collaboration within their organizations. By building strong relationships with their employees, they nurture trust and respect, laying the foundation for effective teamwork. The culture of collaboration and shared purpose they create inspires employees to work together harmoniously towards common goals that have a positive impact.

Conflict resolution is a crucial aspect of peaceful leadership. Instead of resorting to confrontational or aggressive methods, leaders who are spiritual work towards conflict resolution through dialogue and compromise. Their goal is to find solutions that benefit all parties involved, maintaining mutual respect and understanding throughout the process.

Peaceful leaders who are spiritual are driven by compassion and empathy. They possess a deep understanding of their employees' needs and concerns. They work tirelessly to create a workplace culture that cherishes kindness, understanding, and support. By leading with compassion, they inspire their employees to be their best selves, fostering positive change in the world.

Several of the leaders interviewed for this book, who identified as spiritual, recounted experiencing a profound sense of peace as a result of their spiritual practices. These practices, such as prayer and faith, left them feeling serene and calm. Participant 4 described spirituality as a source of balance and inner peace, saying, "It puts me at ease, at peace... and just feeling good."

Peace can be described as a state of tranquility with a calm mind, and it can also represent the absence of both physical and psychological conflict. Religious texts abound with references to peace, underlining its significance. Verses from the Bible, like Isaiah 26:3, assert that keeping one's mind on faith leads to perfect peace. The Quran (5:16) speaks of "the paths of peace," highlighting God's love for peace (2:205). The Sikh Guru Arjan's words emphasize the importance of peace, as he states, "The Merciful Master has now ordained that no one annoys, oppresses, or inflicts pain on another. All shall abide in peace in a benign regime" (GGS p. 74).

Spirituality, which fosters happiness, love, peace, and harmony, significantly influences individual values and beliefs. Karadag's research highlights how these personal values impact organizational culture. Spirituality shapes leaders' values and leadership styles, affecting organizational culture, employee happiness, productivity, and ultimately company profits.

Peace is an influential trait that molds the leadership approach of individuals who are both spiritual and determined to guide their organizations. By creating a serene presence, fostering harmony and collaboration, resolving conflicts peacefully, and leading with compassion and empathy, these leaders can establish a culture of peace and positivity that propels their organizations to success and inspires them to make a positive impact in the world. In the heart of chaos, these leaders are the pillars of tranquility.

◆ ◆ ◆

19. Positivity

Positivity is more than just a mindset; it is a catalyst for change and growth. Leaders who embrace positivity can inspire their teams, enhance productivity, and create a culture of resilience. Positive leadership involves recognizing and leveraging strengths, fostering an optimistic outlook, and encouraging a growth mindset. Research by Smith, Minor, and Brashen in 2018 concluded that positive leaders are more likely to have engaged and motivated teams, leading to better overall performance. The integration of positivity, spirituality, and faith creates a leadership style that is both effective and humane. This holistic approach ensures that leaders are not only focused on achieving goals but also on the well-being of their teams. By combining these elements, leaders can foster an environment of trust, innovation, and sustained growth.

In today's world, the concepts of positivity, spirituality, faith, and leadership are increasingly interconnected. Together, they provide a foundation for addressing challenges and motivating others, serving as an internal guide for decision-making and building resilience. While these concepts can exist independently, their combination creates a unique synergy that enhances personal development and influences those around us. According to participant 2: "Spirituality simply means staying in that state of mind of positive spirit... It doesn't matter what happens - you are always in a balanced state of mind, and you accept things as they come, as the will of God."

Positivity is more than just optimism; it's an intentional outlook on life, grounded in hope and resilience. Research on positive psychology has shown that individuals who maintain a positive outlook can experience better mental health, improved relationships, and increased motivation (Fredrickson, 2001). Leaders who harness positivity foster a culture of openness, creativity, and productivity. These leaders don't ignore challenges; instead, they approach problems with a growth mindset, cultivating an environment where setbacks are viewed as opportunities for growth (Dweck, 2006).

Positive leadership is also directly linked to team performance. When leaders exhibit positivity, they increase employee engagement and reduce stress, fostering an environment where teams feel safe to take risks and innovate (Avolio & Gardner, 2005). Such environments contribute to a sense of collective efficacy, where each individual feels empowered to contribute meaningfully. As an example, Nelson Mandela exemplified positivity in leadership. Despite his long imprisonment, Mandela emerged with a message of reconciliation rather than revenge which also reflects his spirituality and deep faith. His leadership approach inspired a divided nation to work toward unity, highlighting how positive leadership can bring about transformative change.

Integrating positivity, spirituality, and faith in leadership allows leaders to bring their full selves to their roles. Leaders who operate from this holistic perspective cultivate not only their own well-being but also create a nurturing environment for their teams. This form of leadership cultivates trust, encourages both individual and collective development, and enhances the organization's resilience to external pressures (George, 2003). Leaders who prioritize positivity and spirituality often prioritize the development of others as well. They become mentors, focusing on empowering others to discover and pursue their own purpose. In this way, they cultivate future leaders and establish a legacy that extends beyond their individual contributions. An example of this type of leader is Oprah Winfrey who has often spoken about her spiritual journey and commitment to positive leadership. She attributes her resilience and success to her spiritual practices and a deep sense of purpose. Winfrey's leadership style has inspired countless others to prioritize personal growth and seek purpose in their work, demonstrating how positive and spiritual leadership can transform lives.

Integrating positivity, spirituality, faith, and leadership fosters a unique blend of resilience and compassion in individuals and teams. By cultivating these qualities, leaders can create a lasting impact, not only on their immediate environment but also on the lives of those they inspire. The synergy between these elements encourages growth, supports well-being, and ultimately, creates a more fulfilling and purposeful life. As leaders continue on their journeys, they may benefit from confidently leading with positivity, grounded in spirituality and guided by an unwavering faith in their purpose. The synergy of positivity, spirituality, faith, and leadership creates a powerful framework for leading with purpose and compassion. By embracing these elements, leaders can inspire their teams, foster a positive organizational culture, and achieve sustainable success.

◆ ◆ ◆

20. Prayer

Leadership is a dynamic endeavor that demands a multifaceted approach, especially for those who are spiritual. For leaders who are spiritual, prayer serves as a powerful compass. It allows them to pause, reflect on their values, beliefs, and priorities, and gain a deeper understanding of their mission and vision. This newfound clarity and purpose become contagious, inspiring employees to embrace a similar mindset and work collaboratively toward shared goals.

The ability to remain grounded and centered in the face of adversity is a hallmark of spiritual leaders. When confronted with stress or uncertainty, they turn to prayer to find a sense of peace and calm. This inner serenity aids in making sound decisions and maintaining a positive outlook, which is particularly critical during times of crisis when employees look to their leaders for guidance and support.

Prayer becomes a potent instrument for fostering a sense of community and connection among employees. It brings people together and instills a shared sense of purpose and identity. Encouraging employees to pray together creates unity and cohesion, which helps in building a robust organizational culture and promoting a profound sense of belonging.

Prayer encourages leaders who are spiritual to embrace humility and compassion in their leadership style. By acknowledging their own limitations and seeking guidance from a higher power, they prevent themselves from becoming overly self-centered or egotistical in their decision-making. This inclusive and collaborative approach to leadership is invaluable, especially in diverse or multicultural organizations.

The leaders interviewed for this book expressed a profound belief in the efficacy of prayer. They considered prayer as a means of seeking support, blessings, guidance, and forgiveness from God. For many, prayer was more than a practice; it served as a source of comfort, inner peace, and tranquility. Prayer was also a mechanism for alleviating guilt and cognitive dissonance through petitions for forgiveness. Participant 5 illustrated this reliance on prayer by stating that it played a pivotal role in his decision-making process: "I pray in my office, asking God for guidance, questioning Him on what my next decision or step should be... Prayer centers me, making me feel peaceful and calm, and providing me with a sense of consolation."

References to prayer can be found in various religious texts, underscoring its significance. The Bible, for example, in 2 Chronicles 7:14, emphasizes the power of prayer and its potential to heal and renew. The Quran, in Surah Al-An'am (6:162), portrays prayer as an offering to God, similar to Hinduism, Judaism, Sikhism, and other faiths.

Studies on leadership and prayer provide insights into its role as a coping mechanism for leaders and its impact on decision-making. Some leaders admit to praying before making important decisions, even in workplaces where religious practices are discouraged. These findings mirror the experiences of the leaders interviewed for this book who recognize the significance of prayer as a tool for reflection, guidance, and decision-making.

Prayer is a vital practice that profoundly influences how leaders who are spiritual lead and manage their organizations. It helps them stay resolutely focused on their goals and maintain a strong sense of purpose. In moments of adversity, it provides grounding and inspires unity among employees. Prayer also nurtures humility and compassion, contributing to a positive and inspiring organizational culture. Through prayer, these leaders empower their employees to achieve their full potential and make a positive impact in the world.

The power of prayer in leadership is undeniable. It serves as a guiding light, nurturing clarity of purpose, resilience in challenging times, community, and compassion. For leaders who are spiritual, prayer is not just a practice; it's a way of life and a source of inspiration. It ultimately shapes a positive and empowering organizational culture where employees can thrive and leave a lasting, positive impact on the world.

❖ ❖ ❖

21. Relationships

Leaders who are spiritual bring a unique perspective to their roles, driven by a deep connection to their values, beliefs, and purpose. At the core of spiritual leadership is the promotion of empathy and compassion. These leaders strive to understand the needs and concerns of their employees. They actively cultivate a workplace culture that treasures kindness, understanding, and support. Leading with empathy empowers employees to reach their full potential and effect positive change in the world. TheselLeaders recognize the importance of nurturing strong relationships with their employees. They build trust and mutual respect while fostering collaboration and shared purpose. Through these relationships, they inspire individuals to work cohesively toward common goals, creating a powerful impact on the world.

Spiritual leaders uphold a strong commitment to honesty and integrity. They ensure transparency in their decision-making processes and strive to establish a culture that values honesty and accountability. By serving as role models of ethical behavior, they inspire employees to follow suit, thereby shaping a more trustworthy and ethical organizational culture.

Gratitude is a fundamental aspect of how spiritual leaders relate to others. They acknowledge and appreciate the contributions of their employees, expressing their gratitude in meaningful ways. This culture of appreciation fosters a more positive and uplifting workplace environment, leading to increased morale and employee engagement. Participants in the study also described their practice of treating others with empathy and respect, guided by the universal principle of the Golden Rule. This principle, found in various religious texts, underscores treating others as they would like to be treated. The believe in treating others with empathy and respect is demonstrated by Participant 3 whose faith dictated his behavior in the workplace, where he treated others with respect and compassion, aligning his actions with the golden rule: "Treat your neighbor like you want to be treated." He believed in the importance of perspective-taking, especially when dealing with difficult individuals, saying, "I try to put myself in their shoes... and try to come to a solution." Similarly, participant 1 also related to employees with compassion because of his spirituality. His compassion for employees was evident in his commitment to treat them "the way I want to be treated." He supported his staff by mentoring them, helping them grow professionally, and investing in their development, acknowledging that "to achieve the right way, you have to invest in people." Although he prioritized achieving organizational goals, he never lost sight of the importance of treating employees well. He humanized his role as a leader, emphasizing, "I'm not just a title; I'm a person just like you."

The Golden Rule, a principle of reciprocity found in numerous religions and ethical systems, emphasizes treating others as one wishes to be treated. This concept resonates deeply with contemporary leadership theory, particularly concerning the importance of empathy and respect in leader-follower relationships. While the Golden Rule itself is a philosophical tenet, its principles are supported by research in organizational behavior and leadership. For example, a study by Lilius et al. (2008) explored the impact of compassion at work on employee well-being and performance. While not explicitly referencing emotional intelligence and the Golden Rule, the study found that leaders who demonstrate self-awareness, self-regulation, motivation, empathy, and social skills foster a more positive work environment, leading to increased employee satisfaction, commitment, and performance. These findings align with the core tenets of the Golden Rule, suggesting that leaders who prioritize understanding and responding to the emotional needs of their employees create a context where individuals feel valued and respected, thus contributing to organizational success. This echoes the wisdom found in many religious traditions, emphasizing the importance of treating others with compassion and understanding.

Spiritual leaders shape organizations and influence the world through empathy, honesty, and gratitude. By fostering deep relationships and a nurturing culture, they empower others to thrive and lead with purpose. More than a concept, spiritual leadership is a transformative force that leaves a lasting legacy of compassion and ethical values.

◆ ◆ ◆

22. Respect

Respect is fundamental to spiritual leadership. Leaders guided by their faith inherently value respect in all their interactions —with employees, colleagues, and stakeholders—and weave it into the fabric of their organizations. One participant shared: "Because of my religion, I treat my colleagues and those who report to me with respect." This commitment creates an environment where individuals feel valued and can reach their full potential.

Respect fosters trust and transparency. Spiritual leaders genuinely value the opinions, values, and experiences of their team members, building strong rapport and open communication. This transparency empowers employees to voice their ideas and concerns, enabling leaders to make well-informed decisions.

Inclusivity and diversity flourish where respect is paramount. Spiritual leaders appreciate the unique contributions of each individual, creating a workplace where everyone feels respected and valued. This inclusivity fuels creativity, innovation, and productivity, as employees are more willing to share ideas and collaborate.

Respect also promotes accountability. Spiritual leaders not only treat their employees with respect but also hold them accountable for their actions and decisions. This fosters ownership and empowers employees to make a positive impact.

Many faiths, including Christianity and Sikhism, emphasize respect for others in their teachings. These principles guide spiritual leaders, shaping their actions and building respect-based relationships. Research, such as the work of Van Quaquebeke, supports the idea that employees value respectful leadership. Spiritual leaders, often driven by their religious beliefs, consistently demonstrate respect towards their teams, treating everyone as equals regardless of hierarchy. This inherent respect translates into increased employee productivity, performance, and overall satisfaction.

In short, respect profoundly influences spiritual leadership. It nurtures trust, transparency, inclusivity, diversity, and accountability. By prioritizing respect, these leaders create positive, supportive environments where employees thrive and contribute meaningfully to the world. Respect, therefore, is not just a trait but a cornerstone of spiritual leadership, transforming organizations into places where individuals can truly flourish.

◆ ◆ ◆

23. Role Modeling

The impact of role modeling on spiritual leadership cannot be overstated. Spiritual leaders understand the profound importance of leading by example, embodying the values and principles they wish to instill in their organizations. This practice shapes a workplace culture defined by excellence, integrity, and innovation. Participant 8 exemplified role modeling. He led by example, showing qualities such as kindness, generosity, and empathy. "They see in you a kind of person they love to be...Those are Christian principles, but you don't have to label them as such to demonstrate them." He also emphasized the importance of role modeling in appearance, speech, and conduct: "Role modeling includes your appearance, your manner of speech, and your ability to relate to people in decent jokes."

Spiritual leaders recognize that their behavior is constantly observed. They model the behaviors and attitudes they desire to see in their workforce, setting the stage for a culture of excellence and integrity. By demonstrating kindness, compassion, and honesty, they create a ripple effect. Employees, inspired by their leaders' conduct, are more likely to emulate these qualities, fostering a harmonious and productive environment. This aligns with the concept of "being the change you wish to see in the world," often attributed to Mahatma Gandhi, though its exact origin is debated.

Role modeling becomes a powerful tool for inspiring and motivating teams. By embodying core values, leaders demonstrate what can be achieved through dedication and hard work. Employees, observing their leaders' commitment, become inspired to follow suit, resulting in a more engaged and motivated workforce. This resonates with the idea of leaders as "servant leaders," a concept popularized by Robert K. Greenleaf, where leaders prioritize the needs of their followers and empower them.

Role modeling also encourages a culture of learning and growth. By demonstrating a willingness to learn and self-improve, leaders inspire their employees to do the same. When employees witness their leaders engaging in personal and professional development, they are motivated to embark on similar journeys, fostering an innovative and dynamic workplace. This mirrors the Islamic emphasis on seeking knowledge, as exemplified in the saying, "Seeking knowledge is an obligation upon every Muslim."

Furthermore, role modeling builds trust and rapport. When leaders align their behaviors with organizational values, they foster a sense of unity and shared purpose. This engenders loyalty and commitment among employees who feel valued and appreciated. Proverbs 20:7 (NIV) states, "The righteous man walks in his integrity; blessed are his children after him," highlighting the impact of a leader's consistent behavior.

Many spiritual leaders cite religious figures or divine examples as inspiration, acting as role models for their employees in turn. This emulation of worthy values and principles extends from their spiritual beliefs into the workplace. This approach resonates with various religious texts. For example, the Quran (33:21) states, "There has certainly been for you in the Messenger of Allah an excellent example for anyone whose hope is in Allah and the Last Day and who remembers Allah often," highlighting the Prophet Muhammad as a role model for Muslims. Similarly, Hebrews 13:7 (NIV) encourages believers to, "Remember your leaders, who spoke the word of God to you. Consider the outcome of their way of life and imitate their faith."

Research supports the positive influence of role modeling, particularly in spiritual leadership. Studies examining the character-centered and moral leadership of religious figures, like the Prophet Muhammad, suggest the advantages of this approach for leaders in various fields (e.g., Avolio et al., 2009). Other research indicates that positive leadership role modeling improves employee morale and performance, enhances organizational citizenship behaviors, and increases job satisfaction (e.g., Brown et al., 2005).

In summary, role modeling is a cornerstone of spiritual leadership. By embodying cherished values and principles, spiritual leaders inspire excellence, integrity, and innovation. Their commitment to leading by example encourages employees to follow suit, nurturing a work environment characterized by shared purpose, trust, and motivation. Spiritual leaders, acting as beacons of inspiration, create not only healthy workplaces but also pathways to success, profitability, and positive change.

◆ ◆ ◆

24. Salvation

The concept of salvation, a central tenet in many spiritual traditions, refers to deliverance from negative outcomes, often through divine intervention. As one participant noted, "Spirituality also leads us to believe that there is life after death, and man is accountable to either eternal damnation or eternal acceptance into the kingdom of God." This quest for salvation profoundly influences how spiritual leaders lead and manage their organizations.

Spiritual leaders often feel a deep responsibility for the spiritual well-being of their followers, extending their leadership beyond tangible goals to encompass the pursuit of salvation. This responsibility is manifested in many ways. Some adopt a charismatic style, inspiring through personal qualities and spiritual insights, fostering a shared purpose, and encouraging spiritual growth. Others employ a more instructional approach, providing clear guidance and rules, acting as shepherds guiding their flock toward salvation.

Regardless of style, spiritual leaders often base decisions

on a higher moral code or divine guidance, drawing upon scriptures, prayer, or meditation. This emphasis on morality shapes organizational culture. For example, organizations led by Christian leaders might prioritize values like honesty, humility, and service (e.g., Philippians 2:1-11), while those led by Buddhist leaders might emphasize compassion, mindfulness, and non-violence (e.g., the Four Noble Truths).

However, the pursuit of salvation can present challenges. The temptation to use fear or coercion to ensure compliance can create a culture of fear and control. Furthermore, an overemphasis on personal spiritual growth can lead to neglecting practical organizational concerns and stakeholders outside the spiritual community. The cited example of participant 10, the police officer who prioritized his personal code of helping others, even when it conflicted with policy, illustrates this dissonance or tension. This resonates with the struggle between personal conviction and professional duty, a theme explored in various ethical frameworks.

Interviews with spiritual leaders frequently reveal salvation as a primary motivation. For many, it represents deliverance from sin, a path to heaven, and avoidance of damnation. Religious texts, such as the Bible (e.g., Romans 10:9) and the Quran (e.g., 2:186), emphasize avoiding sin and obedience as pathways to salvation. Research suggests that this quest for salvation influences organizational culture, driving moral change and encouraging authentic self-expression (e.g., Fry, 2003). Leaders who openly express their spirituality often foster an atmosphere of integrity and respect, contributing to a positive work environment (e.g., Mitroff & Denton, 1999).

The quest for salvation significantly impacts spiritual leadership. The sense of responsibility for followers' spiritual well-being drives leaders to lead by example and make decisions based on a higher moral code. While this can create a positive and ethical organizational culture, leaders must balance spiritual aspirations with practical organizational needs. Ultimately, the pursuit of salvation plays a profound role in shaping spiritual leadership, influencing organizational culture, and fostering a work environment characterized by integrity, respect, and moral transformation.

◆ ◆ ◆

25. Self-Identity

The intersection of self-identity, leadership, and spirituality offers a powerful framework for understanding effective leadership. Self-identity, encompassing beliefs, values, experiences, and perceptions, forms the bedrock of how individuals interact with the world. A strong self-identity enables confident decision-making, authentic communication, and empathetic leadership. As Kouzes and Posner (2017) suggest, exemplary leadership begins with self-awareness. Leaders who understand their strengths and weaknesses can lead with authenticity and humility, fostering an environment of openness and growth.

The convergence of self-identity, leadership, and spirituality offers fertile ground for growth. Leaders who cultivate a strong sense of self and align their actions with their spiritual beliefs are better equipped to navigate complexity, inspire others, and create positive change. Integrating introspection, mindfulness, and purpose fosters authenticity, empathy, and resilience. This aligns with the idea of "servant leadership" (Greenleaf, 1977), where leaders prioritize the needs of their followers and empower them.

Self-identity is the internal compass guiding a leader's decisions, actions, and interactions. A leader grounded in a strong sense of self can navigate complexities while remaining true to their principles. Spirituality, transcending religious connotations, embodies a deeper connection with one's inner self and the universe, fostering purpose and encouraging transformative leadership.

The convergence of self-identity, leadership, and spirituality manifests in several ways:

• Authenticity: Leaders aligning actions with spiritual and identity-based values are perceived as more authentic, inspiring trust. As Matthew 6:21 (NIV) states, "For where your treasure is, there your heart will be also," suggesting that true authenticity stems from aligning one's actions with their deepest values.

• Resilience: A strong spiritual core bolsters resilience, enabling leaders to withstand challenges. Romans 5:3-5 (NIV) speaks to the power of perseverance and character development through trials.

• Empathy: Spirituality often enhances empathy, allowing leaders to connect deeply and foster inclusive environments. Micah 6:8 (NIV) calls for acting justly, loving mercy, and walking humbly with God, highlighting the importance of empathy and compassion.

Leaders can integrate self-identity with spirituality through:

• Reflection: Regular introspection helps leaders stay connected to core values.

• Mindfulness: Mindfulness enhances presence and attentiveness, leading to thoughtful decision-making.

• Service: A service-oriented mindset reinforces contributing to the greater good. Mark 10:45 (NIV) states, "For even the Son of Man did not come to be served, but to serve, and to give his life as a ransom for many," emphasizing the importance of service in leadership.

Gandhi's leadership, rooted in his Hindu beliefs of ahimsa (non-violence) and satyagraha (truth-force), exemplifies the power of this integration. His strong self-identity, coupled with spiritual convictions, empowered him to lead India to independence. Oprah Winfrey's leadership, guided by her spiritual journey and commitment to personal growth, demonstrates the impact of authenticity and empathy in inspiring others.

The interplay of self-identity, leadership, and spirituality offers a rich tapestry for growth. By embracing introspection, cultivating authenticity, and aligning actions with spiritual beliefs, leaders foster trust, empathy, and purpose. This elevates leadership, inspiring others to reach their full potential. Ultimately, this dynamic process can transform leadership, creating a more compassionate and equitable world.

◆ ◆ ◆

26. Spiritual Connection

A recurring theme in interviews with spiritual leaders is their profound connection with others and the divine. For many, the quest for connectedness with God is a powerful motivator, influencing their behavior, leadership style, and interactions. Phipps (1981) defined spirituality as "the human desire for connection with the transcendent," a concept echoed by Del Rio and White (2000), who described it as "relating to others and seeking unity with the transcendent." This desire shapes behavior, aligning it with faith tenets to maintain connection with the divine. Deviating from these principles can be perceived as sin, creating distance from the divine.

Participant 7's perspective on spirituality is profoundly insightful. She states, "Spirituality is seeking a meaningful connection with someone who is much, much more superior than you; and that is your creator." This seeking of connection is frequently referenced in scripture. John 15:5 (NIV) states, "I am the vine; you are the branches. If you remain in me and I in you, you will bear much fruit; apart from me you can do nothing." This emphasizes the vital connection between believers and God, a concept that aligns with spiritual leadership. According to Quinnine (2007), spiritual leadership is defined as a framework that enables individuals to engage with their spiritual selves, which serve as the foundation for vision, inspiration, values, integrity, and purpose.

Drawing from scripture and research, it's clear that spiritual leaders earnestly seek closeness to their deity. In this pursuit, they adapt their behavior to align with their faith, demonstrating integrity, honesty, and empathy – all essential leadership traits. These qualities directly impact employee engagement and satisfaction, fostering a positive workplace. This aligns with research on authentic leadership, which emphasizes the importance of leaders acting in accordance with their values (Avolio & Gardner, 2005).

The quest for connectedness, like the quest for salvation, can significantly shape spiritual leadership. While these motivations inspire purpose, morality, and commitment, they can also present challenges, such as the potential for fear, coercion, or neglect of practical concerns. Effective spiritual leaders balance spiritual responsibilities with practical obligations, prioritizing the well-being of all stakeholders. This echoes the concept of interpersonal oriented and servant leadership (Greenleaf, 1977), where leaders prioritize the needs of those they lead.

The quest for divine connectedness transcends faith boundaries. It drives spiritual leaders to align their behavior with their faith, maintaining connection with the transcendent. This influences their leadership, fostering integrity, honesty, and empathy, which enhances employee engagement and satisfaction. Balancing this quest with practical leadership concerns is crucial for creating harmonious and effective organizations. Ultimately, the ability to harmonize spiritual and practical responsibilities contributes to a thriving organizational culture.

◆ ◆ ◆

27. Spiritual Experience

Personal spiritual experiences can range from fleeting moments of insight and revelation to extended periods of profound spiritual growth and transformation. Exploration of this impact uncovered both the positive attributes they bring to leadership and the challenges they may present. Leaders who have had personal spiritual experiences often report a heightened sense of purpose and meaning in their roles. They perceive their leadership as a spiritual calling, transcending mere job or career. This profound sense of purpose engenders a deep commitment to the well-being of their organization and all its stakeholders, inspiring leaders to guide with authenticity and fervor.

These spiritual leaders tend to adopt a holistic perspective on leadership. Their responsibilities extend beyond achieving organizational goals to include fostering spiritual growth and well-being in their followers. Consequently, their leadership styles prioritize qualities such as empathy, compassion, and servant leadership. This broader perspective elevates the well-being of individuals within their organization.

Spiritual leaders with personal spiritual experiences often make decisions differently than their counterparts. They may rely on intuition, inner guidance, or divine inspiration as significant factors in their decision-making process, alongside rational analysis, and data. This dual approach results in decisions that are more closely aligned with their personal values and spiritual beliefs, increasing the likelihood of achieving both spiritual and practical objectives.

Despite their positive impact, personal spiritual experiences can present certain challenges. If a leader regards these experiences as the sole valid source of guidance, they might overlook the perspectives of followers and other stakeholders, thereby diminishing diversity of thought and perspective. This limitation can hinder innovation and creativity within the organization. Another challenge stems from the risk of personal spiritual experiences shaping an organizational culture centered around the leader's personal spiritual beliefs, rather than aligning with the needs of the organization and its diverse stakeholders. This narrow focus on specific spiritual traditions or beliefs can lead to a lack of inclusivity.

Leaders interviewed for this book shared descriptions of unique spiritual experiences stemming from their spirituality. These experiences were overwhelmingly positive, characterized by feelings of peace, joy, calmness, and confidence, often occurring during spiritual rituals like prayer and meditation. They also described experiencing answered prayers and sensing the presence of sacred or spiritual forces in their surroundings. These positive experiences serve as powerful motivation for spiritual leaders to continue their spiritual practices and behaviors, translating into improved leadership within their organizations. Participant 5 described deeply moving spiritual experiences that shaped his identity. "Those experiences of God are essential to who I am. If I'm not living that out, I'd want to know how I can better live it in my life." This spiritual experience gave him a sense of peace and purpose, helping him understand his gifts and how to use them for greater good.

These spiritual experiences find references in religious texts, such as Acts (2:4) from the Bible, which states, "And they were all filled with the Holy Spirit and began to speak in other tongues as the Spirit gave them utterance." Sikh scripture similarly emphasizes the role of faith in unlocking spiritual wisdom. Personal spiritual experiences wield a profound influence on how spiritual leaders manage and lead their organizations. They infuse leadership with a deeper sense of purpose, compassion, and well-being, benefiting both leaders and their followers. However, they also bring the challenge of striking a balance between spiritual convictions and practical organizational needs. Effective spiritual leaders can navigate these challenges by embracing diverse perspectives, prioritizing inclusivity, empathy, and remaining open to alternative forms of guidance. This dynamic equilibrium ultimately empowers leaders to serve the holistic well-being of their organizations and all stakeholders.

◆ ◆ ◆

28. Spiritual Guidance

Spiritual guidance plays a significant role in shaping the leadership styles and practices of spiritually inclined leaders. These leaders often utilize prayer, meditation, consultation with mentors, or scriptural insights. While beneficial, spiritual guidance also presents challenges.

One profound influence is the promotion of servant leadership. Leaders seeking spiritual guidance tend to prioritize service to others, fostering a culture of empathy and support. This aligns with Greenleaf's (1977) concept of servant leadership, where leaders prioritize the needs of their followers. Spiritual guidance also influences ethical decision-making. Leaders drawing on spiritual sources often base decisions on moral principles rather than short-term gains, instilling integrity, and trust. This resonates with Brown et al.'s (2005) work on ethical leadership, which emphasizes the importance of moral character and values.

However, overreliance on spiritual guidance can lead to detachment from practical realities, causing leaders to neglect business considerations or miss opportunities. Another challenge is potential dogmatism. Attachment to specific beliefs can stifle innovation and create rigidity. This highlights the importance of balancing spiritual insights with practical considerations, a point emphasized by Fry (2003) in his work on spiritual leadership.

Leaders interviewed for this book shared experiences of seeking spiritual guidance, particularly through prayer, during challenging situations. As one participant noted, "I can't separate my faith from my decision-making... I pray in my office, asking God for guidance, questioning Him on what my next decision or step should be." This resonates with the idea of "divine guidance" found in many religious traditions. Psalm 25:4-5 (NIV), for example, calls for divine guidance and emphasizes truth and hope in God. Similarly, the Quran (e.g., 2:186) emphasizes that guidance from God is a source of healing and mercy.

Research indicates a growing trend of embracing spirituality in the workplace, giving rise to spiritual leadership (e.g., Fry, 2003; Mitroff & Denton, 1999). This model encourages self-consciousness, mindfulness, and service beyond self-interest. Some organizations even incorporate practices like hiring spiritual directors. Spiritual guidance, a core element of spiritual leadership, has been linked to positive organizational outcomes like increased employee commitment, retention, morale, and productivity (e.g., Benefiel, 2003).

Spiritual guidance significantly influences spiritual leaders. It encourages servant leadership and ethical decision-making, fostering empathy and integrity. However, it also presents challenges, such as neglecting practical needs and resisting new ideas. Effective spiritual leaders balance spiritual guidance with practical considerations, remaining open to diverse perspectives and prioritizing stakeholder well-being. They make decisions aligned with both personal values and organizational needs.

◆ ◆ ◆

29. Spiritual Identity

Spiritual identity, encompassing an individual's sense of self and belonging derived from spiritual beliefs, practices, and community, significantly influences leadership. Leaders with a strong need for spiritual identity often view their leadership role as integral to this identity, prioritizing alignment with their beliefs and values as suggested by the social identity and cognitive dissonance theories. This need for spiritual identity often translates into leadership styles emphasizing empathy, compassion, and servant leadership (Greenleaf, 1977).

These leaders tend to make decisions resonating with personal values, viewing their role not just as achieving organizational goals but also as an expression of their spiritual identity. They prioritize spiritual values like love, compassion, and social justice, even when they might not be the most practical or profitable choices. This aligns with the concept of values-based leadership (Brown et al., 2005), where leaders' actions are guided by deeply held principles.

However, over-attachment to spiritual identity can lead to resistance to new ideas or perspectives. Leaders may become defensive or dismissive of feedback, hindering adaptation to changing circumstances. Furthermore, it can create an organizational culture centered on the leader's personal beliefs, potentially limiting inclusivity and diversity. This highlights the importance of self-awareness and the ability to balance personal convictions with organizational needs.

Research participants in this book emphasized their strong identification with their spirituality. One participant stated that her values and spiritual identity are consistent across all aspects of her life. This integrated approach reflects the idea of authentic leadership (Avolio & Gardner, 2005), where leaders demonstrate consistency between their inner values and outward actions.

References to spiritual identity are found in various religious texts. John 15:15 (NIV) describes a shift from servants to friends, symbolizing close identification with faith. Sikhism emphasizes the turban and uncut hair as key identifiers and symbols of commitment. These external symbols reflect an internal commitment, similar to how a leader's actions should reflect their internal values.

The need for spiritual identity significantly affects spiritual leadership. While it inspires commitment to purpose and well-being, it can also create challenges. Effective spiritual leaders balance this need with a commitment to all stakeholders' well-being. They remain open to diverse perspectives, prioritize inclusivity, and make decisions aligning with both personal values and organizational needs. This echoes the call for leaders to be both authentic and adaptable, balancing inner conviction with external realities.

◆ ◆ ◆

30. Trust

Trust is fundamental to effective leadership, especially for spiritual leaders. It is the bedrock upon which respect, accountability, and transparency are built, ultimately driving organizational success. Spiritual leaders understand that trust is reciprocal. They demonstrate trustworthiness through honesty, transparency, and reliability, fostering a culture of openness where followers feel comfortable voicing their opinions and concerns. This aligns with Kouzes and Posner's (2017) work on exemplary leadership, which emphasizes the importance of building trust through consistent and credible actions.

Spiritual leaders often prioritize developing authentic relationships with their followers, investing time to connect personally and demonstrating genuine care which creates a sense of belonging and community, making followers feel valued. Caring for followers resonates with the concept of servant leadership (Greenleaf, 1977), where leaders prioritize the needs of their followers. Established trust significantly influences decision-making. Trusted leaders involve followers in the process, seeking input and prioritizing their needs. This leads to informed and inclusive decisions, cultivating collaboration and shared responsibility. This collaborative approach is supported by research that demonstrates the positive impact of participative leadership on team performance (Somech, 2005).

However, trust is fragile. Betrayal can severely damage an organization, leading to loss of respect, accountability, and transparency, fostering suspicion and division. Spiritual leaders must prioritize preserving trust by consistently upholding honesty and transparency. This aligns with the ethical leadership literature, which highlights the importance of integrity and ethical conduct in building and maintaining trust (Brown et al., 2005). Interviewed leaders emphasized truth as a guiding principle. One participant stated, "If you don't tell me the truth, I won't trust you, and we can't have a strong partnership." Many expressed profound trust in God, extending this trust to others and emphasizing leading trustworthy lives. This resonates with the importance of integrity in spiritual traditions. Proverbs 3:5 (NIV) advises, "Trust in the Lord with all your heart and lean not on your own understanding." Similarly, the Quran 3:159 encourages placing trust in Allah.

Like scriptures, research also supports the link between trust and effective leadership. As David Mineo asserts, "Trust is the bond that connects organizational leaders to their followers or employees, ultimately leading to leadership and overall organizational success." This aligns with another research demonstrating the positive impact of trust on organizational performance (Mayer et al., 1995). Similar to those interviewed for this book, spiritual leaders, often drawing on their faith, extend this trust to their employees thereby creating a positive work environment and fostering success. In short, trust is essential for spiritual leadership. Leaders who build trust create a foundation of respect, accountability, and transparency. By prioritizing relationships, involving followers in decisions, and maintaining honesty, they create a culture of openness where individuals feel valued. Effective spiritual leaders demonstrate trustworthiness and prioritize stakeholder well-being, fostering trust that forms the bedrock of their leadership.

◆ ◆ ◆

CHAPTER SEVEN

The Golden Rule and Leadership

The thirty leadership qualities explored in this book, derived from in-depth interviews with successful leaders across various fields, converge on a central principle: the "golden rule" - treating others as you wish to be treated. This core theme, reflecting the profound influence of spirituality on leadership as articulated by the ten leaders interviewed, resonates deeply with the Christian concept of the "fruit of the Spirit" (Galatians 5:22-23): love, joy, peace, patience, kindness, goodness, faithfulness, gentleness, and self-control. These virtues, while central to Christianity, find parallels in other faiths, including Islam, Buddhism, Hinduism, Sikhism, Judaism, and African traditional religions. This commonality across diverse belief systems underscores the leaders' experiences of how faith shapes their behavior and leadership styles, fostering empathy, compassion, and a deep sense of responsibility towards their followers. While the ten interviewees do not represent the full spectrum of global faiths, the shared emphasis on these virtues across numerous traditions reinforces the universality of the "golden rule," the "fruit of the Spirit," and the thirty leadership qualities discussed in this book, suggesting that these principles are not confined to any one belief system but rather represent a common ground for ethical and effective leadership.

This book explored the intricate relationship between spirituality and leadership style, utilizing Moustakas's (1994) empirical phenomenological approach to analyze data from interviews with ten leaders. The research identified two core elements of the lived experience of spiritual organizational leadership: compassion for others and the possession of core ethical values. These elements, deeply rooted in spirituality, significantly influence decision-making, behavior, and leadership style. The study revealed that spirituality acts as a driving force for these leaders. Participants consistently described themselves as motivated by compassion and ethical values stemming from their spiritual beliefs. This translated into an interpersonal leadership approach, often manifesting as servant or transformational leadership styles, prioritizing people over tasks. The outcome of this study aligns with research by Fry (2003) suggesting a positive relationship between spirituality and servant leadership. Fry's work emphasizes the altruistic and other-centered focus of servant leadership, which resonates with the compassion-driven approach described by the study participants. They prioritize the needs of their followers, empower them, and help them develop their full potential. This approach is often associated with higher levels of employee engagement, satisfaction, and organizational commitment.

Furthermore, the leaders in the study often exhibited characteristics of transformational leadership, inspiring and motivating their followers to achieve shared goals through a compelling vision and a focus on personal growth. This is consistent with the idea that spirituality can provide a sense of purpose and meaning, which can be a powerful motivator for both leaders and followers. However, it's important to note that some research suggests that the relationship between spirituality and leadership styles might be more complex and context-dependent (e.g., Sandage et al., 2010). Sandage et al. found that the expression of spirituality in leadership can vary across diverse cultural and organizational contexts, suggesting that while compassion and ethical values may be common themes, their manifestation in specific leadership behaviors can differ. For example, in some cultures, leaders might express their spirituality through a more directive and authoritative style, while in others, a more collaborative and participative approach might be preferred. Additionally, the specific values emphasized by spiritual leaders can vary depending on their religious or philosophical traditions. Therefore, it's crucial to consider the cultural and contextual factors that might influence the relationship between spirituality and leadership.

The leaders' commitment to core ethical values, such as honesty, fairness, justice, and equality, was deeply ingrained in their spirituality and consistently reflected in their behaviors. Prayer for forgiveness and spiritual guidance were common practices, demonstrating the integration of their faith into their daily lives. This aligns with the concept of moral identity, where individuals' ethical values become central to their self-concept (Aquino & Reed, 2002). When these values clash with organizational norms, as the study suggests, leaders may experience dissonance. To resolve this, they may adjust their behavior to align with their values, potentially shaping their leadership style. This resonates with social identity theory, which posits that individuals strive for consistency between their personal values and their social roles (Tajfel & Turner, 1979). The study's observation about leaders modifying their behavior to reduce dissonance highlights this dynamic. They might engage in behaviors such as whistleblowing, ethical decision-making, or advocating for social justice within the organization. This can lead to a more authentic and values-driven leadership style, which can enhance trust and respect among followers.

However, the study doesn't explore potential negative consequences of this, such as leaders feeling pressured to compromise their beliefs to fit within the organization, which could lead to mental health issues, burnout, or disengagement (e.g., Maslach & Leiter, 2001). Leaders might face challenges such as resistance from colleagues, criticism from superiors, or even legal repercussions for acting on their values. This can be particularly difficult in organizations with a strong emphasis on profit maximization or where ethical concerns are not prioritized. Therefore, it's important to create a supportive organizational culture that values ethical behavior and allows leaders to express their spirituality without fear of reprisal.

The "golden rule" was a recurring theme among the leaders interviewed for this book, guiding their interactions with compassion, tolerance, and respect. This emphasis on interpersonal relationships echoes the findings of other studies that have linked spirituality to positive workplace behaviors (e.g., Benefiel, 2003). Benefiel (2003) argues that spirituality can foster a sense of community and interconnectedness, leading to more ethical and compassionate organizational practices. Leaders who embody the golden rule often create a more inclusive and harmonious work environment, where employees feel valued, respected, and supported. This can lead to improved communication, collaboration, and teamwork, as well as a greater sense of belonging and purpose among employees. Furthermore, it can enhance the organization's reputation and attract and retain top talent.

However, it's crucial to acknowledge that the study's sample size of ten leaders limits the generalizability of these findings. Larger and more diverse samples are needed to explore the nuances of the relationship between spirituality and leadership across different demographics and organizational settings. Future research could investigate how spirituality influences leadership in different industries, organizational sizes, and cultural contexts. It could also explore the role of gender, age, and other demographic factors in shaping the expression of spirituality in leadership.

The participants also integrated spiritual guidance and prayer into their decision-making processes, believing in the power of divine intervention. This reliance on faith-based decision-making aligns with research on religious coping, where individuals use their religious beliefs and practices to manage stress and life challenges (Pargament,

1997). Pargament's (1997) work highlights the numerous ways individuals engage with their faith to navigate difficult situations, including seeking guidance through prayer and relying on a sense of divine support. Leaders might use prayer to seek clarity, discernment, and strength in making important decisions. They might also rely on their faith community for support and guidance. This can provide a sense of peace and confidence in the decision-making process, particularly in situations of uncertainty or ambiguity.

However, the study does not discuss how these leaders reconciled faith-based decision-making with data-driven or evidence-based approaches, which is an important consideration in contemporary organizational leadership. In today's complex and rapidly changing business environment, leaders need to be able to integrate both faith-based intuition and rational analysis in their decision-making. This requires a balanced approach that recognizes the limitations of both approaches and seeks to leverage their strengths. Future research could explore how spiritual leaders integrate faith and reason in their decision-making processes and how this influences organizational outcomes.

The study concludes by emphasizing the importance of understanding the lived experiences of spiritual leaders, particularly how they navigate the challenges of practicing their spirituality in the workplace. It offers valuable insights into the influence of personal spirituality on leadership styles and contributes to the growing body of literature on the intersection of spirituality, leadership, and business. Future research could explore the specific mechanisms through which spirituality influences leadership behaviors, as well as the potential benefits and challenges of incorporating spirituality into organizational culture. Additionally, comparing the experiences of leaders from different religious backgrounds could provide a richer understanding of this complex relationship. It could also investigate the impact of spiritual leadership on organizational performance, employee well-being, and social responsibility.

Understanding The Role Of Spirituality In Leadership

The ten leaders interviewed, despite their diverse religious affiliations and beliefs, shared a common thread: spirituality profoundly influences their leadership styles and behaviors. Their narratives consistently highlighted interpersonal-oriented leadership, compassion, and a strong ethical compass. Beyond the overarching principle of the "golden rule" - treating others as one wishes to be treated - several key themes emerged from their lived experiences:

1. Spirituality as a Guiding Force: All participants emphasized the profound impact of spirituality on their leadership. They demonstrated an unwavering commitment to interpersonal relationships, even while acknowledging the demands of achieving business objectives. Compassion and concern for others, particularly employees and team members, were fundamental drivers of their leadership approach. This manifested in several ways, such as prioritizing employee well-being, fostering a sense of community within the workplace, and actively seeking input and feedback from their teams. They recognized that a supportive and inclusive environment not only benefited their employees but also contributed to the overall success of the organization. In essence, one can say that loving God and loving people can be good for business and organizational success.

2. Spiritual Guidance in Decision-Making: These leaders turned to their spirituality for guidance in critical decisions. Prayer and spiritual practices played a significant role in their work-related choices, providing a framework for ethical, harmonious, and sound judgment. They believed that seeking guidance from a higher power allowed them to make decisions

that were not only in the best interests of the organization but also aligned with their personal values and beliefs. This often involved taking time for reflection and contemplation before making important decisions.

3. Rewards and Consequences: Many believed that aligning with their spirituality brought divine rewards and blessings, while deviating from their beliefs carried consequences. This reinforced the importance of adhering to their spiritual values. This belief system instilled in them a sense of accountability and responsibility, motivating them to act with integrity and make choices that were aligned with their spiritual principles.

4. Feelings of Dissonance: The leaders consistently reported experiencing dissonance, guilt, or conflict when their actions contradicted their spirituality. Avoiding such feelings was central to their leadership approach. This sensitivity to their inner compass ensured that their actions were always in line with their values, fostering a sense of authenticity and integrity in their leadership.

5. Core Ethical Values: A set of core ethical values, closely tied to their spirituality, informed their leadership and business practices. These values included trustworthiness, dependability, respect, fairness, honesty, loyalty, integrity, and gratitude. These values were not merely abstract concepts but rather guiding principles that shaped their behavior and decision-making in all aspects of their professional lives.

6. Gratitude and Forgiveness: Expressing gratitude and seeking forgiveness were integral to their spiritual practices, extending to their relationships with others and reinforcing their commitment to ethical and compassionate leadership. This practice fostered a sense of humility and empathy, allowing them to build strong and meaningful relationships with their colleagues and employees.

7. Leading as Role Models: These leaders understood the

importance of embodying the behaviors they expected from their employees. Their faith and spirituality provided a framework for exemplary leadership. They recognized that their actions spoke louder than words and that their employees were more likely to follow their lead if they demonstrated the values and behaviors they espoused.

8. Motivation and Inspiration: Spirituality and faith motivated and inspired these leaders in both their professional and personal lives, driving them toward a more compassionate and people-centered leadership style. This inner drive fueled their passion for their work and their commitment to making a positive impact on the lives of others.

9. The Search for Salvation: For many, obedience to God was intertwined with the pursuit of salvation, further motivating their commitment to their faith's principles. This belief system provided them with a sense of purpose and direction, guiding their actions and shaping their priorities.

10. Self-Identity and Spiritual Connection: These leaders identified strongly with their spirituality, considering it integral to their sense of self. Their connection with a higher power provided peace, joy, and confidence. This deep sense of connection allowed them to approach their leadership with a sense of calm and assurance, even in the face of challenges and adversity.

11. The Golden Rule in Action: The "golden rule" epitomized the participants' leadership philosophy. They viewed spirituality as the foundation of their ethical behavior, decision-making, and harmonious interactions. This principle guided their actions in all aspects of their leadership, from resolving conflicts to recognizing and rewarding achievements. They strived to create a culture of respect and understanding, where everyone felt valued and heard.

In essence, spirituality is increasingly recognized as a

vital component of effective leadership, fostering a deeper sense of purpose, ethical guidance, and a more human-centered approach. Leaders with well-developed spiritual intelligence are better equipped to navigate complex challenges while maintaining inner peace and upholding ethical conduct. This spiritual intelligence, cultivated through practices like meditation, prayer, or simply mindful reflection, empowers leaders to make values-driven decisions, cultivate compassionate work environments, and contribute positively to the broader community. The consistent theme throughout the participants' narratives is the golden rule, which regardless of their individual religious affiliations, underscores the crucial role of spirituality in fostering compassionate, ethical, and people-centered leadership.

These leaders, drawing strength and inspiration from their spiritual beliefs, consistently prioritize the well-being of their teams, recognizing that a supportive and inclusive environment not only benefits individual employees but also contributes to the overall success of the organization. They understand that true leadership is not about wielding power or authority, but rather about empowering others to reach their full potential. Moreover, these spiritually intelligent leaders are deeply committed to ethical conduct, recognizing that their actions have far-reaching consequences. They strive to make decisions that are not only in the best interests of the organization but also aligned with their personal values and principles. This unwavering commitment to ethical behavior fosters trust and respect among their colleagues, creating a culture of integrity that permeates the entire workplace. Beyond their immediate work environment, these leaders also recognize their responsibility to contribute positively to society. They seek opportunities to use their influence and resources to address social issues, promote sustainability, and make a positive impact on the world around them. This sense of social responsibility is often rooted in their spiritual beliefs, which emphasize the importance of compassion, service, and stewardship.

By embodying and role-modeling these spiritual qualities in their daily interactions and leadership practices, these leaders - irrespective of their faith, religious belief, or affiliation - not only build lasting legacies but also cultivate positive and productive work environments. Their actions inspire others to embrace similar values, creating a ripple effect that extends far beyond the confines of their organizations. Research has demonstrated that such environments, characterized by trust, respect, and a shared sense of purpose, contribute significantly to improved work quality, enhanced employee well-being, and the overall success of organizations. Employees who feel valued, respected, and supported are more likely to be engaged, motivated, and productive. This, in turn, leads to higher levels of innovation, creativity, and collaboration, ultimately driving organizational performance.

The Golden Rule As The Essence Of Spirituality In Leadership

In closing, the golden rule—treating others as you wish to be treated—has proven itself to be more than a mere platitude. It is a foundational principle, a universal truth that transcends time, culture, and creed. As we have explored in these pages, it is the bedrock upon which ethical, compassionate, and truly effective leadership is built. It is the compass that guides leaders through complex ethical dilemmas, the anchor that keeps them grounded in their values, and the bridge that connects them to the hearts and minds of those they lead.

The leaders whose stories and insights have illuminated this book have demonstrated how the golden rule, when sincerely embraced and consistently applied, shapes not only individual character but also organizational culture and societal impact. Their experiences underscore that spirituality, far from being a separate or supplementary aspect of leadership, is in fact the very essence of it. It is the wellspring from which compassion, empathy, integrity, and all the other virtues essential to true leadership flow. It is the quiet voice within that whispers guidance, the inner light that illuminates the path forward, and the unwavering conviction that fuels their commitment to serving others. These leaders, diverse in their backgrounds and beliefs, share a common thread: a deep commitment to treating others with the same respect, fairness, and kindness that they themselves desire. This commitment is not merely a matter of words but is reflected in their actions, their decisions, and their relationships. It is woven into the fabric of their leadership, informing every aspect of how they interact with their teams, their colleagues, and the world at large. It is evident in the way they listen attentively to others' perspectives, the way they celebrate their successes, and the way they support them through challenges. It is apparent in their willingness to admit mistakes, their commitment to transparency, and their unwavering dedication to doing what is right, even when it is difficult.

The golden rule, as we have seen, is not a passive principle but an active force. It requires conscious effort, constant reflection, and a willingness to hold oneself accountable to the highest ethical standards. It demands that leaders not only know what is right but also have the courage to do what is right, even when it is difficult or unpopular. It calls for a deep understanding of oneself, one's values, and one's motivations. It necessitates a willingness to step outside of one's comfort zone, to challenge the status quo, and to advocate for those who are marginalized or oppressed. But the rewards of leading by the golden rule are immeasurable. It fosters trust, builds strong relationships, inspires loyalty, and creates a culture of respect and collaboration. It empowers individuals to reach their full potential, strengthens organizations to achieve their goals, and ultimately contributes to a more just, peaceful, and compassionate world. It creates a ripple effect, inspiring others to embrace the same values and principles, leading to a more harmonious and equitable society. It leaves a legacy that extends far beyond the individual leader, shaping the lives of countless others for generations to come.

As you move forward in your personal or professional life, it is my hope that this book will serve as a reminder of the enduring power of the golden rule. May it inspire you, the reader, to embrace this principle in your own life and leadership, to treat others as you wish to be treated, and to make your own unique contribution to creating a better future for all. May it challenge you to examine your own actions and motivations, to reflect on how you interact with others, and to strive to embody the values of compassion, empathy, and integrity in all that you do. And may it empower you to become a leader who not only achieves great things but also inspires greatness in others.

Bibliography

- American Psychological Association. (2003). Guidelines for Multicultural Education, Training, Research, Practice, and Organizational Change for Psychologists. Washington, DC: Author.
- American Psychological Association. (2010). Ethical Principles and Psychologists Code of Conduct. Retrieved from http://www.apa.org/ethics/code/index.aspx?item=3
- Andronic, G., & Dumitrascu, D. (2017). The relationship between leadership and employees. International Conference Knowledge Based Organization, 23(1).
- Aquino, K., & Reed, A. (2002). The self-importance of moral identity. Journal of Personality and Social Psychology, 83(6), 1423–1440.
- Aronson, E., & Mills, J. (1959). The effect of severity of initiation on liking for a group. Journal of Abnormal and Social Psychology, 59(2), 177–181.
- Astin, H. S. (2004). Some thoughts on the role of spirituality in transformational leadership. Spirituality in Higher Education Newsletter, 1(4).
- Avolio, B. J., Walumbwa, F. O., & Weber, T. J. (2009). Leadership: Current theories, research, and future directions. Annual Review of Psychology, 60, 421-449.
- Awan, S., & Sitwat, A. (2014). Workplace spirituality, self-esteem, and psychological well-being among mental health professionals. Pakistan Journal of Psychological Research, 29(1), 125.
- Avolio, B. J., & Gardner, W. L. (2005). Authentic leadership development: Getting to the root of positive forms of leadership. The Leadership Quarterly, 16(3), 315–338.
- Barrett, R. (1998). Liberating the Corporate Soul: Building a Visionary Organization. Boston, Mass: Routledge.
- Bacha, E., & Walker, S. (2013). The relationship between transformational leadership and followers' perceptions of fairness. Journal of Business Ethics, 116, 667–680. https://doi.org/10.1007/s10551-012-1507-z
- Barrow, J. (n.d.). Sikh spirituality in daily life. Retrieved from Sikh Spirituality in Daily Life (theway.org.uk)

- Bass, B. M., & Riggio, R. E. (2006). Transformational Leadership (2nd ed.). Mahwah, NJ: Lawrence Erlbaum Associates.
- Bass, B. M. (1990). Bass and Stogdill's Handbook of Leadership Theory, Research, and Managerial Applications (3rd ed.). New York: The Free Press.
- Bass, B. M., & Steidlmeier, P. (1999). Ethics, character, and authentic transformational leadership behavior. The Leadership Quarterly, 10(2), 181-217. doi:10.1016/S104 9843(99)00016-8
- Baumsteiger, R., Chenneville, T., & McGuire, J. F. (2013). The roles of religiosity and spirituality in moral reasoning. Ethics & Behavior, 23(4), 266-277. doi:10.1080/10508422.2013.782814
- Beamish, G. (2005). How chief executives learn and what behavior factors distinguish them from other people. Industrial and Commercial Training, 37(3), 138-144. doi:10.1108/00197850510593746
- Beekun, R. I. (2012). Character centered leadership: Muhammad (p) as an ethical role model for CEOs. Journal of Management Development, 31(10), 1003-1020. https://doi.org/10.1108/02621711211281799
- Beekun, R. I., & Westerman, J. W. (2012). Spirituality and national culture as antecedents to ethical decision-making: A comparison between the United States and Norway. Journal of Business Ethics, 110(1), 33-44. doi:10.1007/s10551-0111145-x
- Bell, E. E. (2014). Graduating Black males: A generic qualitative study. Qualitative Report, 19(7), 1-10.
- Benefiel, M. (2003). Mapping the terrain of spiritual leadership. The Leadership Quarterly, 14(2), 169-189.
- Benefiel, M. J. (2003). Spirituality and organizations: A framework for research and practice. Journal of Organizational Change Management, 16(6), 593-610.
- Berger, R. (2015). Now I see it, now I don't: Researcher's position and reflexivity in qualitative research. Qualitative Research, 15(2), 219-234.
- Bonner, C. E. (2007). From coercive to spiritual: What style of leadership is prevalent in K—12 public schools? (Order No. 3256250). Available from ProQuest Dissertations & Theses Global. (304863453). Retrieved

from http://search.proquest.com.library.capella.edu/docview/304863453?accountid=27965

- Broderick, P. C., & Blewitt, P. (2010). The Life Span: Human Development for Helping Professionals (3rd ed.). Boston, MA: Allyn & Bacon. ISBN: 9780137152476.
- Brown, M. E., Treviño, L. K., & Harrison, D. A. (2005). Ethical leadership: A social learning perspective for construct development and testing. Organizational Behavior and Human Decision Processes, 97(2), 117-134.
- Brown, L. M., & Posner, B. Z. (2001). Exploring the relationship between learning and leadership. Leadership & Organization Development Journal, 22(6), 274-280. https://doi.org/10.1108/01437730110403204
- Buie, E., & Blythe, M. (2013). Spirituality: There's an app for that! (But not a lot of research). 2315-2324. doi:10.1145/2468356.2468754
- Burke, R. (2006). Leadership and spirituality. Foresight, 8(6), 14-25. doi:10.1108/14636680610712504
- Cameron, K. S., & Caza, A. (2002). Organizational and leadership virtues and the role of forgiveness. Journal of Leadership and Organizational Studies, 9, 33-48.
- Carroll, P. (2006). Nursing Leadership and Management: A Practical Guide. Clifton Park, NY: Cengage. ISBN: 10:1-4018-2704-7
- Cassar, S., & Shinebourne, P. (2012). What does spirituality mean to you? An interpretative phenomenological analysis of the experience of spirituality. Existential Analysis, 23(1).
- Chang, E. C., Jilani, Z., Yu, T., Fowler, E. E., Lin, J., Webb, J. R., & Hirsch, J. K. (2015). Fundamental dimensions of personality underlying spirituality: Further evidence for the construct validity of the RiTE measure of spirituality. Personality and Individual Differences, 75, 175-178. doi: 10.1016/j.paid.2014.11.027
- Chun, E., & Youn, N. (2014). Spirituality on creative cognition: The roles of feelings of freedom and unconscious thought. Advances in Consumer Research, 42, 779.
- Clark, A. (2006). Language, embodiment, and the cognitive niche. Trends in Cognitive Sciences, 10(8), 370-374. doi: 10.1016/j.tics.2006.06.012

- Cloud, H., & Townsend, J. (2011). Boundaries: When to Say Yes, How to Say No to Take Control of Your Life. Zondervan.
- Cohen, S., Janicki-Deverts, D., & Miller, G. E. (2007). Psychological stress and disease. JAMA, 298(14), 1685–1687.
- Collins, J. (2001). Good to Great: Why Some Companies Make the Leap and Others Don't. HarperCollins Publishers.
- Conger, J. A., & Kanungo, R. N. (1998). Charismatic Leadership in Organizations. Sage Publications.
- Cottrell, P. L. (1987). The Story of Cadbury. Methuen Publishing.
- Covey, S. R. (1989). The 7 Habits of Highly Effective People: Powerful Lessons in Personal Change. Simon and Schuster.
- Covey, S. R. (2006). The Speed of Trust: The One Thing That Changes Everything. Free Press.
- Coy, J. S. (2013). Stories of the accused: A transcendental phenomenological inquiry of family therapists and accusations of unprofessional conduct. (Order No. 3601790, Alliant International University). ProQuest Dissertations and Theses, 161. Retrieved from http://search.proquest.com.library.capella.edu/docview/1468453826?accountid=27965.
- Crabb, L. (2014). Understanding People: Deep Longings for Relationship. Zondervan.
- Ciulla, J. B. (1998). Ethics and leadership effectiveness. Leadership Quarterly, 9(2), 155-166.
- Davidson, R. J., & McEwen, B. S. (2012). Social influences on neuroplasticity: Stress and interventions to promote well-being. Nature Neuroscience, 15(5), 689–695.
- Dent, E. B., Higgins, M. E., & Wharf, D. M. (2005). Spirituality and leadership: An empirical review of definitions, distinctions, and embedded assumptions. The Leadership Quarterly, 16(5), 625-653. doi: 10.1016/j.leaqua.2005.07.002
- Del Rio, C. M., & White, L. J. (2012, March 19). Separating spirituality from religiosity: A holomorphic attitudinal perspective. Psychology of Religion and Spirituality. Advance online publication. doi:10.1037/a002755

- Del Rio, M. H., & White, C. S. (2000). Spirituality and the workplace: A conceptual framework. Journal of Managerial Psychology, 15(7), 681-692.
- DePaulo, B. M. (1992). Nonverbal behavior and self-presentation. Psychological Bulletin, 111(2), 203-243. doi:10.1037/0033-2909.111.2.203
- De Vries, R. E., Bakker-Pieper, A., & Oostenveld, W. (2010). Leadership = communication? The relations of leaders' communication styles with leadership styles, knowledge sharing and leadership outcomes. Journal of Business and Psychology, 25(3), 367-380. doi:10.1007/s10869-009-9140-2
- Dutton, J. E., & Heaphy, E. D. (2003). The power of high-quality connections. In Positive Organizational Scholarship (pp. 263-278). Berrett-Koehler Publishers.
- Dweck, C. S. (2006). Mindset: The New Psychology of Success. Random House.
- Eagly, A. H., & Johnson, B. T. (1990). Gender and leadership style: A meta-analysis. Psychological Bulletin, 108(2), 233-256. doi:10.1037/00332909.108.2.233
- Ellison, C. G. (1991). Religious involvement and subjective well-being. Journal of Health and Social Behavior, 32(1), 80-99.
- Emmons, R. A. (2004). The psychology of gratitude: An introduction. In R. A. Emmons & M. E. McCullough (Eds.), Series in affective science. The Psychology of Gratitude (pp. 3–16). Oxford University Press. https://doi.org/10.1093/acprof:oso/9780195150100.003.0001
- Emmons, R. A. (2005). Striving for the sacred: Personal goals, life meaning, and religion. Journal of Psychology and Christianity, 24(1), 21-28.
- Emmons, R. A., & McCullough, M. E. (2003). Counting blessings versus burdens: An experimental investigation of gratitude and subjective well-being in daily life. Journal of Personality and Social Psychology, 84(2), 377–389.
- Fahlberg, L. L., & Fahlberg, L. A. (1991). Exploring spirituality and consciousness with an expanded science: Beyond the ego with empiricism, phenomenology, and contemplation. American Journal of Health Promotion: AJHP, 5(4), 273-281. doi:10.4278/0890-1171-5.4.273
- Fernando, M., & Jackson, B. (2006). The influence

of religion-based workplace spirituality on business leaders' decision-making: An inter-faith study. Journal of Management and Organization, 12(1), 23.

- Festinger, L. (1954). A theory of social comparison processes. Human Relations, 7(2), 117-140. doi:10.1177/001872675400700202
- Festinger, L. (1957). A theory of cognitive dissonance. Stanford, CA: Stanford University Press.
- Festinger, L. (1962). Cognitive dissonance. Scientific American, 207(4), 93-107.
- Festinger, L., & Carlsmith, J. M. (1959). Cognitive consequences of forced compliance. Journal of Abnormal and Social Psychology, 58(2), 203-210. doi:10.1037/h0041593
- Fincham, A. (2019). Cadbury's ethics and the spirit of corporate social responsibility. In N. Burton, & R. Turnbull (Eds.), Quakers, Business and Corporate Responsibility. CSR, Sustainability, Ethics & Governance. Springer, Cham. https://doi.org/10.1007/978-3-030-04034-5_4
- Fluker, W. E. (2008). Spirituality, ethics, and leadership. Spirituality in Higher Education Newsletter, 4(3).
- Ford, G. G. (2006). Ethical Reasoning for Mental Health Professionals. Thousand Oaks, CA: Sage. ISBN: 9780761930945.
- Fredrickson, B. L. (2001). The role of positive emotions in positive psychology: The broaden-and-build theory of positive emotions. American Psychologist, 56(3), 218–226.
- Freed, E. X. (1978). Humanistic psychology (book). Journal of Personality Assessment, 42(6), 656-657. doi:10.1207/s15327752jpa4206_22
- Fry, L. W. (2003). Toward a theory of spiritual leadership. The Leadership Quarterly, 14(6), 693-727. doi: 10.1016/j.leaqua.2003.09.001
- Fry, L. W. (2008). Spiritual leadership: State-of-the-art and future directions for theory, research, and practice. In J. Biberman, & L. Tischler (Eds.), Spirituality in Business. Palgrave Macmillan, New York. https://doi.org/10.1057/9780230611887_7
- Fuller, R. C. (2007). Spirituality in the flesh: The role

of discrete emotions in religious life. *Journal of the American Academy of Religion, 75*(1), 25-51.

- Garg, N., & Gera, S. (2019). Gratitude and leadership in higher education institutions: Exploring the mediating role of social intelligence among teachers. *Journal of Applied Research in Higher Education.* Advance online publication. https://doi.org/10.1108/JARHE-09-2019-0241

- Gary, K. (2006). Spirituality, critical thinking, and the desire for what is infinite. *Studies in Philosophy and Education, 25*(4), 315-326. https://doi.org/10.1007/s11217-006-9008-0

- Gladwell, M. (2005). *Blink: The power of thinking without thinking.* Little, Brown.

- George, B. (2003). *Authentic leadership: Rediscovering the secrets to creating lasting value.* Jossey-Bass.

- Giltinane, C. L. (2013). Leadership styles and theories. *Nursing Standard, 27*(41), 35-39.

- Giorgi, A. (1997). The theory, practice, and evaluation of the phenomenological method as qualitative research. *Journal of Phenomenological Psychology, 28*(2), 235-260.

- Giorgi, A. (2012). The descriptive phenomenological psychological method. *Journal of Phenomenological Psychology, 43*(1), 3-12. https://doi.org/10.1163/156916212X632934

- Goleman, D. (1995). *Emotional intelligence: Why it can matter more than IQ.* Bantam.

- Goodman, J. (2014). Altruism and the golden rule. *Zygon, 49*(2), 381-395. https://doi.org/10.1111/zygo.12089

- Grant, A. M. (2006). A personal perspective on professional coaching and the development of coaching. *Coaching Review, 1*(1), 12-22.

- Gregory Stone, A., Russell, R. F., & Patterson, K. (2004). Transformational versus servant leadership: A difference in leader focus. *Leadership & Organization Development Journal, 25*(4), 349-361. https://doi.org/10.1108/01437730410538671

- Greenleaf, R. K. (1970). *The servant as leader.* Greenleaf Center for Servant Leadership.

- Greenleaf, R. K. (1977). *Servant leadership: A journey into the nature of legitimate power and greatness.* Paulist Press.

- Greenleaf, R. K. (2002). *Servant leadership: A journey into the nature of legitimate power and greatness* (25th Anniversary ed.). Paulist Press.

- Gunbayi, I. (2005). Women and men teachers' approaches to leadership styles. *Social Behavior and Personality: An International Journal, 33*(7), 685-698. https://doi.org/10.2224/sbp.2005.33.7.685

- Hackman, J. R., & Johnson, C. E. (2009). *Leadership: A communication perspective.* Sage Publications.

- Harris, A. E. (2009). Coaching: A new frontier, some questions, and answers. Retrieved from http://www.apait.org/apait/resources/articles/coaching.pdf.

- Hofmann, S. G., Asnaani, A., Vonk, I. J. J., Sawyer, A. T., & Fang, A. (2012). The efficacy of cognitive behavioral therapy: A review of meta-analyses. *Cognitive Therapy and Research, 36*(5), 427-440.

- Hill, P. C., & Pargament, K. I. (2003). Advances in the conceptualization and measurement of religion and spirituality. *American Psychologist, 58*(1), 64-74.

- Hinrichs, K. T. (2007). Follower propensity to commit crimes of obedience: The role of leadership beliefs. *Journal of Leadership & Organizational Studies, 14*(1), 69-76. https://doi.org/10.1177/1071791907304225

- House, R. J. (1996). Path-goal theory of leadership: Lessons, Legacy, and a reformulated theory. *Leadership Quarterly, 7*(3), 323-352.

- Hays, P. A. (2008). Looking into the clinician's mirror: Cultural self-assessment. In P. A. Hays (Ed.), *Addressing cultural complexities in practice: Assessment, diagnosis, and therapy* (2nd ed., pp. 41-62). American Psychological Association.

- Kassin, S., Fein, S., & Markus, H. (2011). *Social psychology* (8th ed.). Wadsworth, Cengage Learning.

- Kavar, L. (2012). *The integrated self: A holistic approach to spirituality and mental health practice.* US: John Hunt Publishing.

- Kavar, L. F. (2015). Spirituality and the sense of self: An inductive analysis. *The Qualitative Report, 20*(5), 696-710. Retrieved from http://www.nova.edu/ssss/QR/QR20/5/kavar8.pdf

- Kiecolt-Glaser, J. K., McGuire, L., Robles, T. F., & Glaser, R. (2002). Emotions, morbidity, and mortality: New perspectives from psychoneuroimmunology. *Annual Review of Psychology, 53*, 83-107.

- Kirkpatrick, S. A., & Locke, E. A. (1991). Leadership: Do traits matter? *Academy of Management Perspectives, 5*(2). https://doi.org/10.5465/ame.1991.4274679

- Koenig, H. G. (2017). Spirituality in patients with chronic illnesses. *Mayo Clinic Proceedings, 92*(7), 1089-1098.

- Kouzes, J. M., & Posner, B. Z. (2007). *The leadership challenge* (4th ed.). John Wiley & Sons.

- Kouzes, J. M., & Posner, B. Z. (2011). *Credibility: How leaders gain and lose it, why people demand it.* Jossey-

Bass.

- Leedy, P. D., & Ormrod, J. E. (2013). *Practical research: Planning and design* (10th ed.). Pearson.

- Lilius, J. M., Worline, M. C., Maitlis, S., Kanov, J., Dutton, J. E., & Frost, P. (2008). *The contours and consequences of compassion at work.* Journal of Organizational Behavior, 29(2), 193–218. https://doi.org/10.1002/job.508

- Maslow, A. H. (1943). A theory of human motivation. *Psychological Review, 50*(4), 370-396. https://doi.org/10.1037/h0054346

- Northouse, P. G. (2018). *Leadership: Theory and practice* (8th ed.). Sage Publications.

- Palmer, P. J. (2004). *A hidden wholeness: The journey toward an undivided life.* Jossey-Bass.

- Pargament, K. I. (1997). *The psychology of religion and coping: Theory, research, practice.* Guilford Press.

- Percy, W. H., Kostere, K., & Kostere, S. (2015). Generic qualitative research in psychology. *The Qualitative Report, 20*(2), 76-85.

- Pew Research Center. (2014). *America's changing religious landscape.*

- Phipps, K. A. (2012). Spirituality and strategic leadership: The influence of spiritual beliefs on strategic decision making. *Journal of Business Ethics, 106*(2), 177-189. https://doi.org/10.1007/s10551-011-0988-5

- Powell, L. H., Shahabi, L., & Thoresen, C. E. (2003). Religion and spirituality: Linkages to physical health. *American Psychologist, 58*(1), 36-52. https://doi.org/10.1037/0003-066X.58.1.36

- Punia, B. K., & Yadav, P. (2015). Predictive estimates of employees' intelligence at workplace with special reference to emotional and spiritual intelligence. *BVICAM's International Journal of Information Technology, 7*(1), 845-852.

- Quinnine, T. E. (2007). *Spiritual leadership within the service industry: A phenomenological study interpreting the spiritual leadership experiences of eight business executives* (Order No. 3264282). ProQuest Dissertations & Theses Global. https://search.proquest.com/docview/304720553

- Raskin, J. D. (2012). Evolutionary constructivism and humanistic psychology. *Journal of Theoretical and Philosophical Psychology, 32*(2), 119-133. https://doi.org/10.1037/a0025158

- Reave, L. (2005). Spiritual values and practices related to leadership effectiveness. *The Leadership Quarterly, 16*(5), 655-687. https://doi.org/10.1016/j.leaqua.2005.07.003

- Riebel, L. (1982). Humanistic psychology: How realistic? *Small Group Research, 13*(3), 349-371. https://doi.org/10.1177/104649648201300306

- Roslow, S. (1940). Nation-wide and local validation of the P.Q. or personality quotient test. *Journal of Applied Psychology, 24*(5), 529-539. https://doi.org/10.1037/h0061608

- Rowe, B. D. (2013). It IS about chicken: Chick-fil-A, post-humanist intersectionality, and gastro-aesthetic pedagogy. *Journal of Thought, 48*(2), 89.

- Sandage, S. J., Hill, P. C., & Veenstra, L. (2010). Spiritual leadership: A review and conceptual framework. *The Leadership Quarterly, 21*(4), 600-619.

- Seaward, B. L. (1995). Reflections of human spirituality for the worksite. *American Journal of Health Promotion, 9*(3), 165-168.

- Schroeder, K. (2000). Black self-esteem. *The*

Education Digest, 65(8), 73.

- Service, R. W., & Carson, C. M. (2009). Management and leadership: Religion the "mother of all context". *Interbeing, 3*(1), 37.

- Shadish, W. R., Cook, T. D., & Campbell, D. T. (2002). *Experimental and quasi-experimental designs for generalized causal inference* (2nd ed.). Wadsworth.

- Shaffer, L. S. (2005). From mirror self-recognition to the looking-glass self: Exploring the justification hypothesis. *Journal of Clinical Psychology, 61*(1), 47-65. https://doi.org/10.1002/jclp.20090

- Sharma, S., & Agarwala, S. (2014). Self-esteem and collective self-esteem as predictors of depression. *Journal of Behavioural Sciences, 24*(1), 21.

- Simon, M. K., & Goes, J. (2011). What is phenomenological research? Retrieved from http://dissertationrecipes.com/wp-content/uploads/2011/04/Phenomenological_Research.pdf.

- Smith, G., Minor, M., & Brashen, H. (2018). *Spiritual leadership: A guide to a leadership style that embraces multiple perspectives.* ERIC.

- Somech, A. (2005). Participative leadership: A means to empower teachers. *Educational Administration Quarterly, 41*(5), 726-752.

- Sweeney, P. J., & Fry, L. W. (2012). Character development through spiritual leadership. *Consulting Psychology Journal: Practice and Research, 64*(2), 89-107.

- Szasz, T. S. (1960). The myth of mental illness. *American Psychologist, 15*(2), 113-118. https://doi.org/10.1037/h0046535

- Tajfel, H. (1982). Social psychology of intergroup relations. *Annual Review of Psychology, 33*(1), 1-39.

https://doi.org/10.1146/annurev.ps.33.020182.000245

- Tajfel, H. (1974). Social identity and intergroup behavior. *Social Science Information, 13*(2), 5-93. https://doi.org/10.1177/053901847401300204
- Tajfel, H., & Turner, J. C. (1979). An integrative theory of intergroup conflict. *The Social Psychology of Intergroup Relations, 33*(47), 7-24.
- Tee, S., Chin, S., Anantharaman, R. N., Yoon, D., & Tong, K. (2011). The roles of emotional intelligence and spiritual intelligence at the workplace. *Journal of Human Resources Management Research, 2011*(2011), 1-9. https://doi.org/10.5171/2011.582992
- The Holy Bible, New International Version (NIV).
- Torrance, H. (2012). Triangulation, respondent validation, and democratic participation in mixed methods research. *Journal of Mixed Methods Research, 6*(2), 111-123.
- U.S. Department of Health and Human Services. (1979). *Belmont Report.* Retrieved from http://www.hhs.gov/ohrp/humansubjects/guidance/belmont.html.
- Van Quaquebeke, N. (2011). Defining respectful leadership. *RSM Insight, 5*, 12-14.
- Vasconcelos, A. F. (2009). Intuition, prayer, and managerial decision-making processes: A religion-based framework. *Management Decision, 47*(6), 930-949. https://doi.org/10.1108/00251740910966668
- Williams, R. (2012). Why every CEO needs a coach, in wired for success. Retrieved from http://www.psychologytoday.com/blog/wired-success/201208/why-every-CEO-needs-coach.

- Williams, J. A., Roberts, C., & Bosselman, R. (2011). Youth sports and the emergence of chameleon leadership. *Journal of Leadership Studies, 5*(3), 6-12. https://doi.org/10.1002/jls.20227
- Winter, G. (2000). A comparative discussion of the notion of validity in qualitative and quantitative research. *The Qualitative Report, 4*(3,4). Retrieved from http://www.nova.edu/ssss/QR/QR4-3/winter.html.
- Worthington, E. L., & Scherer, M. (2004). Forgiveness is an emotion-focused coping strategy that can reduce health risks and promote health resilience: Theory, review, and hypotheses. *Psychology & Health, 19*(3), 385-405.
- Wright, T. L., & Gorsuch, R. L. (1997). Religion, spirituality, and growth. *Journal of Adult Development, 4*(2), 93-101.
- Yasuno, M. (2008). The role of spirituality in leadership for social change. *Spirituality in Higher Education Newsletter, 4*(3), 1-8.
- Yooyanyong, P., & Muenjohn, N. (2010). Leadership styles of expatriate managers: A comparison between American and Japanese expatriates. *Journal of American Academy of Business, Cambridge, 15*(2), 161-167.
- Yukl, G. (2013). *Leadership in organizations* (8th ed.). Pearson.
- Zeigler-Hill, V. (2007). Contingent self-esteem and race: Implications for the Black self-esteem advantage. *Journal of Black Psychology, 33*(1), 51-74.
- Zeigler-Hill, V., & Myers, E. M. (2011). An implicit theory of self-esteem: The consequences of perceived self-esteem for romantic desirability. *Evolutionary Psychology, 9*(2), 147.

- Zwart, G. A. (2000). *The relationship between spirituality and transformational leadership in public, private, and nonprofit sector organizations* (Order No. 9977752). ProQuest Dissertations & Theses Global. https://search.proquest.com/docview/304647564

ABOUT THE AUTHOR

D r. Adeniran Koko is a multifaceted professional with over two decades of experience spanning the healthcare and financial industries. He is a distinguished psychologist, wellness coach, consultant, and scientist dedicated to enhancing both individual and organizational well-being.

Dr. Koko's academic credentials include a Ph.D. in Psychology, an MBA with a specialization in Healthcare Administration, and an MSc in Microbiology. This diverse educational background provides him with a unique perspective on health, wellness, and organizational dynamics. He is a Board-certified Clinical Laboratory Scientist (CLS) and an American Society for Clinical Pathology (ASCP)-certified Medical Laboratory Scientist (MLS), demonstrating his deep understanding of medical science. Further underscoring his expertise, he holds certifications as a Project Management Professional (PMP-PMI), a Lean Six Sigma Black Belt Professional (LBBP), and an Associate Certified Coach (ACC-ICF).

Dr. Koko's professional journey includes serving as the Chief Executive Officer and co-founder of Palm Springs Wellness, a prominent wellness and anti-aging clinic in Southern California. Under his leadership, the clinic has experienced rapid growth and become recognized for its innovative approach to health and wellness. In addition to his business ventures, Dr. Koko is passionate about coaching and mentoring. He maintains a private coaching psychology practice in California, empowering individuals and organizations to reach their full potential.

His commitment to serving the community is evident in his role as the Chief Executive Officer (CEO) and Chairperson of the Nigerian American Public Affairs Committee (NAPAC) Foundation, where he leads initiatives that promote growth and advancement of communities in need. A devoted husband and father of two, Dr. Koko's involvement in various community initiatives focused on social responsibility, education, food security, health, economic empowerment, and community development reflects his strong belief in giving back and making a positive impact on the world around him.

Dr. Koko's career is not just a testament to his academic and professional achievements but also to his unwavering commitment to the betterment of society. His holistic approach to health and wellness, combined with his dedication to community service, continues to inspire and uplift those around him.

www.ingramcontent.com/pod-product-compliance
Lightning Source LLC
LaVergne TN
LVHW041317080426
835513LV00008B/495